Elmer and Me

Kenneth L. Miller

AuthorHouse™
1663 Liberty Drive
Bloomington, IN 47403
www.authorhouse.com
Phone: 1-800-839-8640

First published by AuthorHouse 5/12/2011

ISBN: 978-1-4567-4923-1 (e)
ISBN: 978-1-4567-4922-4 (sc)

Library of Congress Control Number: 2011904821

Printed in the United States of America

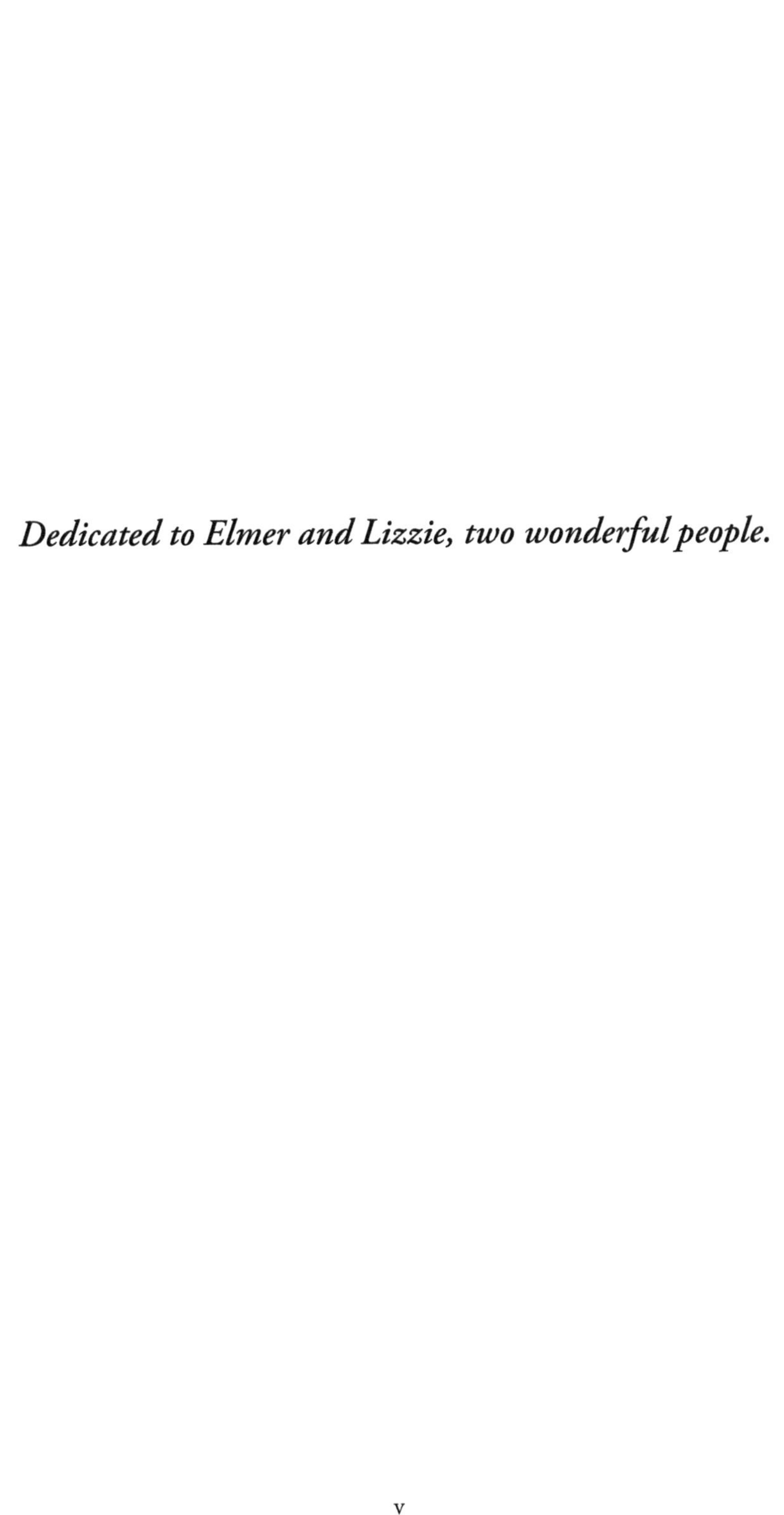

Dedicated to Elmer and Lizzie, two wonderful people.

Acknowledgements:

My wife, Carole for tolerating me as I was going through these adventures and for proof reading each story as it was written.

Jen Roessler and Sharon Hebl for proof readings and encouragement.

Louis Rubin for sharing many of these adventures and always coming back for more.

Arlene Jones for proof reading and offering encouragement.

Some of the stories printed here have previously been published in HPNews. They are reprinted here with permission from the Health Physics Society.

Table of Contents

Elmer on His Tractor

Elmer

NOT LONG AFTER MOVING to Hershey, my wife, Carole, and I made the decision that this would be a great place to live and raise our two sons, Scott and Jeff. We began looking around for a building lot on which to build our new house. Late one afternoon my wife called to say that she had found the perfect building lot and asked if I could meet her there right after work. As we drove up to what would become our future home site in the pristine farm country outside of Hershey, Pennsylvania, I knew immediately that this was the lot that we wanted. There were several dozen Canada geese foraging among the corn stubbles on the lot and just across the road there was a beautiful Pennsylvania Dutch farm.

The day finally arrived when we had the house completed and we could move in. As we were unloading our furniture, Elmer, who owned the farm across the way, pulled into the driveway on his beat up old tractor that was held together with spit and a generous helping of baling wire. He didn't get off the tractor so I walked over and asked him how he was doing. "You're really gonna do it?" he said. "What do you mean?" I asked. "Ya got her finished and yer moving in," he replied. "Yep," I replied. "Is that a freezer I see on your truck?" he asked. "Yes," I replied. "When you get ready to fill it with good beef, let me know," he said. "I'll do that," I replied. "Do you like sweet corn?" he asked. "Yeah, we sure do," I said. "I'll drop some off for you" he said as he started his tractor which coughed and sputtered and belched a huge puff of smoke.

The next evening when I got home from work there were approximately 300 ears of corn sitting in front of our door. Carole and

I were up till the wee small hours of the morning blanching, cutting corn off the cob and bagging it for the freezer.

In the spring Elmer again pulled his tractor into the driveway. "You planning on having a garden?" he asked. "Well, I would sure like to," I answered. "But, I don't have any tools for working a garden as yet," I replied. "I'll be by to plow you up a garden," he said as he began backing out of the driveway. The next afternoon, my wife called to tell me that Elmer had been by to plow my garden. "That's great," I said with enthusiasm. "You're not going to believe it when you see it," she said. "What do you mean?" I asked. "Just wait until you get home and see for yourself," she said as she hung up the phone. That evening, when I got home, I walked out back and could not believe what I saw. Elmer had plowed up a whole acre! As I stood there with my mouth agape, Elmer walked around the house and asked, "What do you think?" "Elmer, what in the world am I going to do with a garden that big?" I asked. "I don't have any tools except a rake and a hoe." "Don't worry, I'll help you" was his reply. Elmer's idea of helping was to disk up the garden for me and to use his corn planter to plant 64 rows of sweet corn. That took up half of my new garden. Someone at work suggested that I try zucchini. So, I planted 20 mounds of zucchini. Since I had so much space to fill, I also planted 20 mounds of cantaloupe, three dozen tomato plants, six rows of green beans, four different kinds of cucumbers, etc. etc. etc. For the rest of the summer, I was a slave to that garden. Every evening I was out in the garden in a futile attempt to beat back the weeds with my trusty hoe. Then, it was the end of summer. Every evening I was out in the garden hauling out produce. Forget about a garden basket, I bought the largest wheelbarrow I could find and I still couldn't haul it all out. After canning hundreds of quarts of tomatoes, pickles, pickle relish and red beets and, filling the freezer with corn, peas and green beans, my wife said that if I planted another garden that big, she would see me in divorce court. It got so that even friends would step into doorways or turn and walk the other way if they saw me coming. I just couldn't give away enough stuff from the garden.

When you mix a physicist with a Pennsylvania Dutch farmer, some interesting things are bound to happen and, they did!

A Raccoon in the Chimney

Every once in a while we need to get away from our professional lives and do something different just to relax, unwind and recharge the old enthusiasm batteries. One Friday in May, I decided to do just that. I took the afternoon off so my fishing buddy, Lou, and I could go up to the cabin and fish the evening hatch. I had the car all packed and was eagerly awaiting Lou's arrival from Maryland so we could be off as it was a 90-mile drive to the cabin. If traffic wasn't too heavy, we would have just enough time to get to the cabin, unpack and head out to the stream in time for the evening hatch to begin and the trout to start feeding.

I was anxiously pacing in my driveway when I spotted Lou's car turning off the highway and onto our road. "Great! We're going to make it," I thought. Just then, Carole, my wife called out to me and told me that Elmer was on the phone. Elmer was my friend. Unfortunately, he had an uncanny knack for calling me at all the wrong times to ask me to help him solve one of his many problems. "What does he want?" I asked. "He said he needs your help in getting a raccoon out of his chimney," she said. "What?" I asked. "Here, you talk to him," she said. I answered the phone and Elmer asked his usual question, "Ken, are you busy?"

"Elmer, Lou and I are just about to leave for the cabin to catch the evening hatch," I told him. "Come on over," was his reply. "Why, what is going on?" I asked. "A raccoon fell down the chimney and I need your help in getting it out," said Elmer. "Elmer, how do you know there is a raccoon in your chimney?" "I can hear it hissing and scuffing around," he said. "Come on over and help me get it out; it won't take long."

Elmer's farmhouse was built in the late 1800s. The kitchen contains one of those open fireplaces where kettles of food were once hung from iron racks for cooking. Years ago Lizzie, Elmer's wife, decided that it was an eyesore, a source of dirt and something that she would never again use for cooking their meals. So, at her insistence, Elmer had a carpenter come in and panel the inside of the fireplace. He kept an old chest of drawers in the opening and, over the years, it had become his treasure chest for everything he had in his pockets when he came in from working on his tractor or puttering around in his barn. To say that it was bulging at the seams would be an understatement. It was filled with nuts, bolts, bent nails, bladeless pocketknives, twists of twine and other things, some that were beyond recognition.

When Lou and I walked up on the porch, Elmer met us at the door. Lizzie was pacing in her dining room, wringing her hands. "Come here and listen," Elmer told us. Before we could do that, we had to move Elmer's treasure chest out of the way. We did so carefully lest it fall apart and we would have to spend the evening rebuilding it for him. Once we got the chest out of the way, no easy task because it weighed a ton, we still could not hear anything. "Wait," Elmer said. "Let me tap on the panel at the top and you'll see what I mean." He gave the panel a sharp rap with his knuckles and, sure enough, we could hear hissing and a scurrying sound above the panel. "Uh oh, now what are we going to do?" I asked as thoughts of being attacked by a raccoon, and possibly one that was rabid, suddenly filled my mind. "No problem," said Elmer, "here, take my 22 rifle and shoot up through the panel a few times." "When we know it's dead, we'll take the panel off and get it out." "Elmer, I don't know if that is such a good idea," I told him. "Here, let me loosen just an edge of the panel and see if I can see what is in there with the flashlight," I suggested. Using a screwdriver from Elmer's chest of drawers, I gently pried the front edge of the panel down just enough so I could shine the flashlight into the opening.

When I shined the flashlight into the opening four large eyes lased out at me; and, their owners made an ungodly hissing sound. I was so startled that I reflexively jerked back and, in so doing, caught my shirt cuff on a nail protruding from the paneling. The next thing I knew, I was lying on my back on the kitchen floor, barely able to see for the cloud of dust surrounding me. On my legs lay the paneling from the top of the fireplace along with half a dozen chimney bricks and an ever-growing mound of soot, sand and other unidentifiable debris that had accumulated in the chimney over the years. On my chest were two half-grown barn owls that seemed to think that I was a special treat their momma had dropped down the chimney for them. When I turned my head, I had a sinking feeling as I caught a glimpse of the cloud of soot that was drifting toward Lizzie who was sitting in her rocking chair in the dining room.

I learned several lessons that afternoon:

- Barn owls will build nests in abandoned chimneys.
- Baby barn owls can fall down the chimney if they are not careful.
- Half-grown barn owls can break your skin.
- It takes five hours to clean soot out of Lizzie's dining room and kitchen.
- When Elmer calls and asks if I am busy, say, "YES!"
- "It won't take long" has a different meaning when you are close to 80.

We never did make it up to the cabin that weekend.

Doing Things the Hard Way

WELL, THE INCIDENT WITH Elmer and the barn owls kept Lou and me from going to the cabin for our weekend of trout fishing. But, once we finally got a chance to kick back and relax, our resolve to do so returned. We agreed to do it the very next Friday. The ensuing week went by slowly, but Friday finally came. Once again I was loading my car in anticipation of Lou's arrival when my wife called out to tell me that Elmer was on the phone. "Oh no, can't you tell him I'm out of town or something?" was my reply. "Sorry, I won't lie to him for you. Here, you talk to him," she said. As Yogi said, "Déjà vu, all over again!" When I answered the phone, my good buddy, Elmer, my PA Dutch farmer neighbor, uttered the words I dreaded, "Ken, are you busy?" "Elmer, Lou and I are just about to leave for the cabin," I said. "Come on over was his reply." "Why, what is the problem?" I asked. "There's a big starling nest in my gutter that is causing the rain to overflow into my attic when it rains," was his reply. "Come on over, this won't take long," he said. "You can reach it from the porch roof. All you have to do is pull it out of the gutter and you and Lou can be on your way. But, don't forget to bring me back some of those good rainbow trout."

"If I'm not back by the time that Lou gets here, send him over to Elmer's," I told my wife. "See you in a couple of days," was her reply.

Elmer's farmhouse, like his barn, is built on a grade. In the back, you walk in on the first floor. In the front, you can walk directly into the basement or, go up a flight of steps to the porch that runs the entire length of the house and allows you to enter the first floor. So, in the front, the rain gutter is three stories above the ground. But, as Elmer pointed out to me, all I had to do was go out a second floor window, onto the porch roof and I could reach up and pull the bird nest out of the gutter. Elmer's theories about jobs were always like that, "no problem, it will only take a minute."

So, in order to get the job over with so I could be on my way, I went up to the front bedroom, opened the window and stepped out onto the porch roof. Now, this is where Elmer's theory of the facility of a job ends with reality! His porch roof is made out of corrugated tin. And, on that day, with the temperature in the mid-eighties, that corrugated, slanting roof turned out to be as slippery as any old greased pig. As soon as I stepped out onto it, I began to slide. I dove for the window and managed to get a good hold on the sill so I could pull myself upright again. Elmer poked his head out to advise me. "Just hold onto the gutter and inch your way over to the nest and reach up and pull it out," he instructed. As I did so, I realized that part of his water problem was due to the fact that his gutter had rusted through beneath the bird's nest. The nest and all the other debris in the gutter looked like it would be enough to fill a bushel basket! I finally inched my way over to it. However, the nest was just about at the limit of my reach. Standing on the slanted roof while holding onto the gutter with one hand and reaching over my head, groping in the dark for the nest created a precarious position. No sooner did my hand make contact with the nest then my feet started slipping. The next thing that I knew was that the gutter had broken allowing the nest and all the other debris to fall on my head with a goodly portion going down the neck of my shirt. However, I didn't have time to worry about that as the gutter bent out from the house and I started slipping further down the roof. Not wanting to slip down and go over the edge of the roof, which was two stories above the ground below, I hurriedly started climbing the bending gutter while issuing a silent prayer that it didn't tear away from the house completely. My heart leapt to my throat as I heard the next fastener in line give way and I began sliding some more. Fortunately, the rest of the gutter held and I was able to inch my way up to the second bedroom window and hang onto the sill. My fingernails were digging into the wood of the sill as I waited for Elmer to find a putty knife so he could crack the paint around the window and raise it.

Fortunately, Lou arrived and got the window open. I was a mess. A bushel of crud had just run down my neck and, to make matters worse, that bird's nest in the gutter had backed up about five gallons of water, all of which had also gone down my neck. Here I was, all ready to leave for a weekend of R&R and some badly needed fly fishing and, I looked like something that had just crawled out of a landfill. To make matters worse, Elmer's gutter was hanging from the roof in pieces. How could I just walk off and leave him with the mess?

Lou suggested that he would run out and get a replacement gutter and we could pop it back in and still get to the cabin late, in time to salvage the weekend. That's when Elmer spoke up and said, "Nope, you won't find any of that kind of gutter, they don't make it any more." Elmer's gutter was the curved, half-cylinder type that sat in special brackets that were made just for it. "Well then, what are we going to do?" I asked. "We'll have to replace it with the kind like you have on your house," he said. "Are you sure that is what you want?" I asked him. "Yep, that'll do it," he said. "OK, Lou, I will take some measurement and while you run to the lumberyard for gutter, I will get the roof edge ready," I said. This time, we tied a rope around my waist and Lou kept tension on it from inside the bedroom, just in case! As I was measuring along the roof edge I came to a spot that looked all dry-rotted. When I poked it with my finger, my finger went right through it. "Elmer, we will have to replace the fascia before we can put up new gutters," I told him. "Yep, do it," was his reply. "What about those cast iron hangers?" I asked. "You'll have to cut them down," Elmer stated. Well, that was easier said than done! A hacksaw wouldn't do it. It took a long handled bolt cutter, which, of course, I had to buy and which has been in my workshop ever since.

You cannot put up new wood without taking the old wood down. And, you cannot attach gutters to new wood without giving it at least a primer coat and one or more finish coats of paint. You cannot put up the new gutter until the paint dries. What with one thing and another, it was Sunday evening before we were standing on the ground admiring the bright new gutter and down spouting. Elmer wasn't satisfied until we got out a water hose and sprayed the roof just so he could see water run out of the bottom end of the down spout. As Lou left Sunday evening, he muttered, "I didn't really want to go fishing any way!"

Epilogue: Several months later, I was at the local hardware store buying some fencing material. When I went into the back room with the clerk, the rain gutter racks caught my eye. There before me were three racks of gutters identical to what Elmer had had on his house. One was in galvanized steel, one was in enameled steel and one was in white plastic. I said to the clerk "I thought they didn't make that type any more?" "Oh we always keep a supply of that on hand for people fixing up old houses," was his reply.

The Old Man and the Lake

Raccoons in the Bushes

Bill rented half of Elmer's farmhouse. For months, he had been regaling Elmer with stories of the incredible fishing where he grew up on Black Lake in New York. Finally, Elmer decided that we all just had to go see where Bill grew up and experience some of that extraordinary fishing. I'm still not quite sure how my friend Lou and I got talked into going along on the trip!

Black Lake is way up in the northernmost part of New York, about a nine-hour drive from Hershey. During the entire nine hours, Elmer chattered away like an excited little kid as he was anticipating catching everything from bass to northern pike. Of course, Bill's accounts of monster walleyes didn't do a thing to lessen Elmer's enthusiasm. Elmer vowed that he was going to take a cooler full of fish home for his great grandchildren and Lizzie, all of whom "just loved fish."

At long last, we arrived at the lake and settled into a cabin owned by a lady that Bill had known while growing up. It was actually in a most incredible, pastoral, setting, with the cabin right on the shore of the lake. We even had two row boats at our disposal for the days that we would be there.

We had arrived at the cabin about seven in the evening. After unloading the car and choosing bedrooms it was time to make our plans for the next couple of days. Since Elmer and Bill were both into spinning gear, we thought it best to pair them up. Lou and I had brought only fly fishing gear, so we formed the second team.

To kick back and relax after such a long and tiring trip would have been the sensible thing to do. But, Elmer would hear none of that. He didn't get to take a vacation from his farm work very often, so he was determined to get in as much fishing as possible on this trip. Bill said that he would row Elmer around the shoreline and let him hook into a northern. Lou and I decided, "What the heck," we might as well take the other boat and see if we could find anything that might be interested in our hula poppers.

Lou and I rowed our boat in the opposite direction from Elmer and Bill. As we neared a cove we began spotting large number of blue gills. Great big bluegills! The granddaddy's of all blue gills! They were huge! Well, at least huge by blue gill standards - meaning they were about the size of your hand. We quit rowing and rigged our fly rods. On the very first cast, a big, fat blue gill came right up out of the water to take the offering. Over the next hour or so, we got carried away! Before we knew it, the bottom of the boat was covered with fish! Just before dark, Lou said "Maybe we ought to call it a night since we are the ones who will probably have to clean all these fish for Elmer."

We rowed the boat back to the cabin to see how Elmer and Bill had made out in their quest for northern pike along the shoreline. When we arrived at the dock, Elmer and Bill were there to meet us. They had not caught any northern pike, but they did have a dozen or so crappies that Bill had cleaned and said we could have for breakfast. Elmer wasn't too keen on eating any of the fish we caught as he told us that he had promised to take some home to Lizzie "After all, she let me come on this trip and, she will be disappointed if I don't take any fish home for her," When we showed him what we had in our boat he replied, "Boy, oh boy, oh boy, you guys hooked into a mess of em. Let's get them cleaned and into the ice chest." So, we filled several large buckets with fish and headed for the cleaning table behind the cabin.

We quickly learned that Elmer's idea of cleaning fish was that he would supervise and comment about how nice each one was and hand us another one as soon as we finished with the one we were cleaning. When cleaning blue gills, the simple way is to filet them. Not so for Elmer, he wanted Lizzie and the kids to be able to see the fish. That meant that each one had to be scaled, not an easy task when it comes to blue gills. By the light of a Coleman lantern, we cleaned fish well into the night. Around midnight, we were getting tired and we still couldn't see the bottoms of the buckets. So, when Elmer wasn't looking, we would occasionally throw a smaller fish into the bushes! After all,

Bill had told us that Black Lake had a healthy raccoon population and, they would appreciate and clean up anything we left them from the fish cleaning. At last, we finally came to the last fish. When it was done and they were all on ice, we headed to bed. The last thing that Lou whispered to me before heading to his bed was "Tomorrow, we throw them back; I never cleaned so many fish in my life!"

The next morning, Bill, Lou and I were sitting around the breakfast table, enjoying our second cups of coffee when Elmer finally emerged from his bedroom. "How did you sleep, Elmer?" I asked. "Didn't get much sleep at all – there were raccoons fighting over something back in the bushes all night! I can't imagine what they were after," was his reply. "Hey, you guys ready to go back out fishing?"

The Lawn Mower

OUR HOUSE IS CENTRALLY located on a two-acre lot. When Carole and I tell people that we built our house, we mean that we really built it in that we did nearly all the work ourselves. As we were in the construction phase, we kept adding things to the plans so that by the time the house was ready to be occupied, we were pretty strapped for cash. Most people who build a house have their preliminary landscaping completed before they move in. In our case, we were so busy with the construction that we didn't have time or money to do much with the lawn, initially. In fact, I didn't even bother with spreading grass seed. That didn't matter, since the yard quickly turned green – mostly due to all the weeds that began to grow there. I had a theory about weeds not being able to withstand a lot of mowing and decided to let the lawn seed itself naturally. I figured that with repeated mowing the weeds would die out and the indigenous grasses would soon take over. The only lawn mower that I had at the time was a gas-powered reel mower that my father picked up for me for $2.00 at a yard sale. It worked fine but twenty inch swaths made for a long day (or days) of mowing on a two-acre lot! I vowed that as soon as I could afford it I would buy a decent mower. Well, one day while accompanying Carole to the local store for bedspreads, I spotted a 30 inch riding mower that was on sale. Oh my, the thing dreams are made of! A 30 inch mowing deck on a riding lawn mower! My mind began to quickly compute the time I was going to save on lawn mowing. I just had to have that beauty!

To my chagrin, I quickly learned that even at 30 inches per pass, it takes a long time to mow a two-acre lot! I also learned that cheaper mowers don't hold up well on rough lawns. Nearly every mowing required some repair to that mower as the rough ground vibrated everything loose that could come loose and then some! I quickly began longing for a real riding lawn mower. One day while mowing, I noticed my neighbor mowing his lawn with a bright new orange mower that was several sizes larger than the one I had been using. Mine looked like a toy compared to his. He didn't do me any favors by letting me try his – I knew immediately that I had to have one. A heavy duty mower with a 48 inch mowing deck! A dream- come-true! Sometimes you have to wonder if you are ever truly satisfied! That orange mower certainly reduced my mowing time and made lawn mowing fun – at least for a while. But, I found myself eventually pining for something that would do the job even faster. One day I just happened to find myself in the local lawn mower specialty shop and discovered that they had a beautiful green lawn mower with a sixty-inch mowing deck and a power-flow grass catcher, on sale. That was it! I placed my order before leaving the place. They told me that because of the sale they couldn't take trade-ins but they agreed to sell my orange mower for me and give me the money.

Before my new, green mower could be delivered, Elmer called and asked, "Ken, do you know anything about lawn mower engines?" I gave him my usual reply, "Elmer, the only thing I know about lawn mowers is how to ride them!" "Come on over and take a look at mine – I can't get it started," was his reply. Elmer's lawn mower was a riding lawn mower too. But it was not like mine, the kind that looks like a tractor. His engine was in the rear and the front was just a deck with the steering wheel, clutch and brake and a place for your feet. It was so old that it looked like the only thing holding it together was the many coats of ugly mustard colored paint that had been used on it years ago. The bearings or bushings in the little front wheels were so worn that both leaned when it was sitting and flopped back and forth on the axels, making it vibrate, when you drove it. That didn't matter to Elmer who never replaced anything and felt that "There's still a few more mowings in it." After a new spark plug and replacement of a cracked and leaking gas line we were ready to give it a try. I hopped on and told Elmer to give the starter rope a pull. He did and it started right off. "How do you make this thing go?" I asked him. "Push in the clutch and shift er into gear" was his reply. So, I depressed the clutch and shifted it into gear thinking that I would make a pass around his yard to see how it was running and if the blades needed to be sharpened. Fortunately, Elmer was standing behind me for when I popped out the clutch, that mower did a wheelie, with the front end coming off the ground like a rearing bronco and the rear wheels driving it forward. The next thing I knew, sparks were flying! That lawn mower, pointing skyward, surged forward and only stopped when it encountered Lizzie's metal clothes line post! And, the blade was striking the pole and shooting off sparks like a pin wheel on the Fourth of July! Elmer came running over, flipped the key off and said, "I forgot to tell you, that clutch grabs a little - so, you have to let it out real slow when you are taking off!" "Taking off? If that thing had wings I'd be going past the Harrisburg Airport by now!" I replied. "Elmer, that thing isn't safe to ride – it could kill someone!" I said. "Well, it takes a little getting used to," he said.

That afternoon, I drove my orange riding lawn mower over and gave it to Elmer. "What the hang is this?" he asked. "A present for you," I said. "You're going to kill yourself with that old mower. I am having a new mower delivered tomorrow and don't need this one any more. Send your old one to the scrap heap and use this one from now on." "That old one still works fine," he said. "Why, since you tuned it up, it runs like a new one." This time I wasn't going to take NO for an answer! "Have fun," I said as I turned and headed for home. When I got to my driveway, I turned around and looked over at the farm. Elmer was going back and forth across his lawn – on his old lawn mower! I never did see him using the orange lawn mower so, one day I asked him about it. "I guess I'm just too old to learn something new. That lawn mower of yours is too complicated for me to use. But, the great grandkids sure enjoy riding it around when they come over!" was his reply.

The Plumbing Job

As I was growing up I had a propensity for jumping into things without giving them too much forethought. My mother used to always admonish me "Sometimes you're better off leaving well enough alone!" These words came back to haunt me on many occasions and, especially one day when I found myself doing a plumbing job for Elmer.

The farm house that Elmer and Lizzie lived in was originally built by Elmer's father around 1870. It was typical of the farmhouses of that day in that, like their barns they chose to build them on a slope with entry from the back directly onto the first floor and in the front, you could enter the basement floor or lower section. The house was a duplex, or two-family home, with both halves being two-stories high in the back and three in the front. Typically, the owner lived in one half and the other was either rented out, usually to the top farm hand, or lived in by the eldest son who would one day inherit the farm. The steps going from the kitchens to the basement were usually steep and narrow. Often they were directly under the steps leading to the second floor, which often made a right angle bend after about four to six steps. So, the steps going to the basement ran in parallel with the steps to the second floor. Because of the bend, they were narrow and a number the steps were triangular shaped.

One day as I watched Lizzie struggling to carry a load of laundry down the steps, I jumped up and insisted on giving her a hand. When I got to the basement, I noticed that she was still washing clothes in a 50's model washing machine, the kind that had an agitator tub and a ringer over it. When the clothes were through being washed, they had to be fed, by hand, through the wringer rollers to get as much of the water out as possible.

When I returned to the kitchen I suggested to Elmer that he should consider getting Lizzie a modern washing machine and having it installed in the kitchen so she didn't have to risk falling going up and down the cellar steps. "Well, I could do that but, there ain't no water or electrical lines running to that corner of the kitchen over there. I don't know who the hang I could get to put them in," was his reply. "That wouldn't take much, I could do it for you," I offered. "Good, you get the stuff you'll need and I'll have Shirley take Lizzie out for a washing machine," he said.

Well, Shirley, their daughter, took Lizzie out to the store and they picked out an automatic washing machine that wouldn't be too complicated for Lizzie to use. The day it was delivered, Elmer called to tell me it was ready for me to hook up.

I went to the local hardware and picked out everything that I thought I would need for running the electrical and plumbing lines. The job shouldn't take very long, I thought. It was a simple matter of drilling three holes through the floor, two for the copper water lines and one for the electrical conduit. All three lines would mount to the wall behind the washing machine.

In the basement I soon discovered that Elmer only had one shut-off valve between his well pump and the entire house. That valve hadn't been closed in years and wasn't about to be closed now. The only solution was to shut off the water pump, drain the pressure tank and replace the valve. That required another trip to the hardware store for a new valve and extra fittings. Once I cut the old valve out of the line, I found that their acidic well water had slowly dissolved the inside of the water lines to the point where they could be crushed with your fingers. So, back I went to the hardware store for more copper tubing and more fittings. The next thing that I discovered was that the copper tubing that was still solid had developed an oxide coating on the outside that resisted cleaning and rejected the solder and paste used in connecting sections together. So, back to the hardware store for more tubing and fittings! Fortunately, the plumbing to the second floor was more recent than that to the first floor and did not have to be replaced. Lizzie explained that it wasn't all that long ago that they had put in the plumbing to the second floor. The reason being, that Elmer had resisted, for the longest time, the idea of having a bathtub and an indoor commode in the house. Elmer always felt that if the outhouse was good enough for his parents, it ought to be good enough for them!

The most challenging part of the plumbing job came when connecting the elbows to turn the plumbing up through the floor to the kitchen. The spot chosen was along a basement wall that contained the opening for their coal delivery. They heated the house with hard coal that was almond sized and fed automatically into the furnace by an enclosed augur system. So, under the coal access the coal was piled high and sloped downward and away from the wall. "It's OK, you can stand on the coal and reach er," was Elmer's comment. I got everything measured, prepped and ready to go. However, when I stood on the incline of coal and tried to heat the line so I could solder them together, the coal began sliding out from under my feet. In order to stay where I needed to be, I had to keep stepping forward. By the time I had the joints hot enough to apply the solder I was running in place! Fortunately, when I applied the solder to the joints, it quickly got sucked in and made good seals. I was nearly done with the job, but, my shoes were full of coal and I was a filthy mess! Twelve hours after I started, we were able to turn the water and electricity on and test the washing machine. It was all worth it, to see the look on Lizzie's face – a modern washing machine and no more lugging the laundry up and down those steep steps! And, no more putting the clothes through a wringer! When I got home, Carole asked "What did you do, fall down Elmer's cellar steps?"

About a week later, Elmer called. "You know, you're gonna have to come over and hook up one of those clothes dryers for Lizzie." "How come?" I asked. "Cause, if you don't, she's gonna have to carry the wet clothes down the cellar step to get them out to the clothes line that's in front of the house!"

The Channel Catfish

My son, Jeff, was a typical Huck Finn character. As he was growing up, there wasn't anything that he didn't develop an interest in and, just as quickly abandon to move on to some new interest or adventure. Thus, we went through the usual hobbies with him, including the raising of tropical fish. My wife and I weren't keen to the fact that he wanted to buy an aquarium and begin to breed guppies. Nevertheless, his persistent requests, entrepreneurial dreams and a solemn oath to earn all the money for this new adventure left us with little to object to. Within a few months we had a large aquarium in our den with all the air bubblers, castles, imitation kelp and rock clusters that are typical of the true tropical fish hobbyist. For a while, there was great enthusiasm accompanied by the Miller Chauffer Service making uncountable trips to the pet store for more supplies and often, more fish.

However, as such things will, interest in this newest undertaking waned just like all the rest. Occasionally this led to confrontations between son and mom as the algae level of the tank made it impossible to observe or even count the fish. Mom wasn't impressed by the arguments that the algae was a good source of food for the fish or that the little critters that fed on it became food for the fish. Who would have ever guessed that Elmer would inadvertently solve this problem?

Elmer was always bugging me about taking him fishing. Every time I saw him I knew I would hear, "When are we going to go fishing?" or, "When are we going to take your boat out again?" Finally, the day came when I just had to take another break from work and the constant dealing with problems. That evening it rained. When it was over, I called Elmer and told him that I had been out in the rain and had caught a whole coffee can full of night crawlers. I asked him if he wanted to go fishing in the morning. His answer was the same as could be expected from a kid in a candy store who was asked if he would like a free peppermint stick! So, the next morning, I loaded my boat with tackle, hitched the boat to the car, picked up Elmer and we headed for the Susquehanna River. The bass weren't very active, but the channel catfish were! Before long we had gone through the entire can of night crawlers and the live well on my boat was literally teeming with channel catfish (Elmer never wanted to throw anything back). I had one tiny shred of bait left on my hook and I told Elmer that I was going to see just what I could catch with it before quitting. After a few minutes, the line started to move ever so gently through the water. I set the hook, thinking that I was about to snag yet another monster cat. Instead, when I jerked on the rod, the line come flying up out of the water and a channel catfish of about six inches went flying over my head and into the water on the other side of the boat. "What the hang you got this time?" said Elmer. "A minnow" was my reply. I was actually a little embarrassed when I reeled in my line and had such a small fish dangling from the end. "Keep him," Elmer said. "Elmer, we can't keep such a small fish," I told him. "Nope, keep him. I'm going to put all these fish in the little pond. I'll feed them and Lizzie and me will have a ready supply of fish any time we get hungry for a good mess of fish," he said. "OK", I said, "If that's what you want."

When we got to Elmer's farm we used a net to retrieve the fish from the live well and put them in a bucket of water to transfer them to Elmer's little pond. The last fish remaining was the little one I had caught last. When Elmer saw him in the net, he said "Don't put that one in the pond, the bigger ones will only eat him." "What do you want me to do with it?" I asked. "Take it home and put it in Jeff's aquarium until it gets a little bigger," was his suggestion. So, I did. Channel catfish are magnificent creatures, akin to miniature sharks. They are all silvery with beautiful spots and those incredible whiskers that are typical of the species. At long last, we had a respectable fish in the aquarium! Not one of those wimpy guppies that know nothing except how to produce more guppies! After about three weeks, my wife said "I think the number of fish in the aquarium is decreasing," and "That catfish sure seems to be growing!" My reply was the usual, "hmmmm." After six weeks my wife said, "Take a look at this." "The catfish is the only thing in the tank!" "Hmmmm," I said. "And, that catfish seems to have doubled in size!" she said. "Hmmmm," I said. "Get it out of there and take it over to Elmer's pond," she said. So, I did.

About another three weeks went by and one day I heard my son scream "Mooooom, what happened to all my fish?"

K.MILLER
©2003

The Gray Fox

Initially, our building lot was totally devoid of trees. It had been part of a farm field until the lady who owned it got to where she needed to enter a nursing home. So the small farm was divided up into sizeable lots and sold so she could afford her extended care. Shortly after our house was finished and we moved in, I began looking for trees to line the driveway. I have always been partial to pin oaks and they grew wild in the woods at the back of Elmer's farm which was just across the road from our house. Elmer said that I could dig up and transfer all the pin oaks that I wanted. So, with time my driveway and the front of the lot were lined with pin oaks. The oaks thrived in my soil and as soon as they had their root systems reestablished, they began to grow. After several years they were of a size that some of their limbs were sticking out into my driveway and in need of pruning.

One June day, I was in the process of lopping off lower limbs of the pin oaks when Elmer pulled into my driveway. "Come with me, we're going to shoot a gray fox," he said. "Where," I asked. "Just over here in the back field," was his reply. Now, to a farmer who raises chickens and ducks for sale, a fox of any color is a hated enemy, to be destroyed whenever encountered. It wasn't so much that Elmer raised chickens and ducks, but Lizzie, his wife did. And if Lizzie said that a fox was making off with any of her chickens or ducks, war was declared.

"Do I need a gun?" I asked. "Nope, I've got my 22 rifle in the car," said Elmer. So, I got in and we drove out the dirt road to his back field. "Where did you see the fox?" I asked. "Right up there on the hill where those sumacs are growing," He said. "I want to get a good clean shot at this one so I can get it mounted and put it in the living room for Lizzie. That way whenever she mentions, "fox", I can point to it and tell her I'll take care of it just like I did this one," he explained. We parked the car and began sneaking out through the field. Bent over, we got to the top of the rise and hid behind some scrub brush. "Let's just hunker down here and wait," he whispered. "It'll be along soon."

We sat there for close to a half hour before I caught movement out of the corner of my eye. As I slowly turned my head so as not to spook whatever was moving through the grass, I caught a glimpse of the fox. It was indeed a gray fox and, a magnificent creature. I nudged Elmer and pointed in the direction that I had seen it. Elmer whispered, "I'll wait until it gets into the opening so I have a clean shot." Elmer eased the safety off the gun and rested the barrel over a small limb. The fox took a tentative step into the opening and Elmer fired. I knew it was a clean miss as I saw the puff of dust that was created when the bullet struck the ground several yards beyond the fox. The fox leapt into the air, came down and disappeared. "I got him!" said Elmer. "I don't think so," I told him. "Nope, I got him, let's go down and get him," he said.

When we got to the spot where the fox had been, there was no fox in sight. "I don't see how I could have missed him," Elmer said. "Let's look around for blood." At the side of this small open area there were several groundhog holes. I walked over to have a look at them. There, just inside one of the holes, I could see the fox's tail. He had apparently responded to the shot by seeking to hide in one of the groundhog holes. "Over here, Elmer," I said. "Yep, boy, I knew I got him," he said when he saw the tail. "Elmer, I don't think you hit it," I said. "Now what are we going to do?" "Pull him out," was his reply. "Pull him out? Elmer, he's still alive," I told him. "It doesn't matter, you pull him out far enough so I can shoot him," he said. "Elmer, I'm not so sure that I like this idea," I told him. "Don't worry, I'll shoot him before his head comes out," he said. "All right, but you shoot him before he has a chance to bite me," I told him. "Yep, you just get him out part way and I will take care of him," he said.

Well, like they say, "The best laid plans -----." I grabbed the fox's tail and started to pull. From within the hole came a growling that let me know that the fox wasn't too happy about what I was doing. "Elmer, he's pretty mad," I said. "Don't worry, soon as you get him out here, I'll pop him," was his reply. Well, for a while, it was a pretty even match, me against the fox. But, eventually, I began to make ground and the fox slowly started to come my way. I had the back legs out and said to Elmer, "OK, get ready, here he comes." On my next tug, the fox started to turn around and its head popped out of the hole with jaws agape and that head aimed directly at me. "Whaugh!" Elmer exclaimed as he turned and started running away.

Well, my life didn't exactly flash before my eyes, but it only took a microsecond to realize that I had a real problem on my hands, or in them. I did the only thing I could think of; I immediately started turning and twirling. That did the trick. There I was twirling around and the centrifugal force was keeping that fox aimed out and away from me. After about six turns I still didn't know what I was going to do to end this situation so, I simply let go. Well, Mr. Fox went flying through the air and hit the ground rolling. When he got up, he started walking off like a drunken sailor. The twirling had made him dizzy! Elmer came running up gasping and said, "I thought you were a gonner that time! Now I'll get him." Elmer raised the rifle to take aim. I put my hand on the barrel of the gun and pushed it down. "Elmer, let him go, he's earned the right to go on living," I said. "No, he'll get Lizzie's chickens," he said. But, by then the fox was out of sight.

Over the remainder of that summer, Elmer reminded me several times that "It still spites me that we let that fox get away!" One day that fall I walked down to my mailbox to get the mail and I looked out across Elmer's field. There along the hedgerow was the fox along with his misses and three half-grown youngsters. The mother and the kids quickly disappeared into the underbrush, but he stood and looked at me. He was beautiful! I did an imaginary tip of my hat to him and said, "Nice family." I swear that he winked at me before turning and following his family into the underbrush.

The Northern Pike

ELMER HAD A FRIEND who lived nearby by the name of Joe. Like Elmer, Joe loved to go fishing. But, Joe did all of his fishing in Canada where he was able to catch northern pike. Northern pike are a great game fish. They are voracious predators that are easy to catch and they grow to respectable size, usually in the twenty to fifty inch range while weighing several pounds, with some growing to exceed twenty pounds. Joe was forever tormenting Elmer with tales about the huge northern pike he kept catching on his trips to Canada. However, no matter how often Elmer attempted to invite himself along on one of those trips it never seemed to be the appropriate time for Joe to take Elmer along. Perhaps Joe knew Elmer quite well!

My parents also loved taking fishing trips to Canada to fish for bass and northern pike. They usually made the trip to Canada two or three times each year. After years of stories and home movies about the great fishing they always encountered on their trips, Carole and I and our two sons, Scott and Jeff, joined my parents on one of their trips to Canada. The place where they stayed was pastoral but extremely rustic with single and double roomed cabins sided with rough-cut sawmill lumber that had never seen a paintbrush. The cabins were equipped with crude gas stoves for cooking but little else in the way of amenities. The domestic water source was an old hand-cranked well pump in the front yard that required priming before each use and, the bathroom facilities were provide by an outhouse in the back yard. Our cabin even came complete with a family of three bats living amongst the roof rafters! The only thing that kept the week from being a disaster was the fact that on that particular trip (as with any other fishing trip I took with her) Carole caught the biggest fish!

For several years I listened to Elmer tell about Joe and the big northern pike he always caught on his trips to Canada. In a moment of weakness, I heard myself saying, “Elmer, would you like to go to Canada fishing?” A silly question and once it was out, there was no taking it back! To Canada, with Elmer, I had to go.

At that particular time, my mother was having some health problems that prevented her from traveling great distances. I knew that my father had been missing his fishing trips to Canada and would jump at the chance to return there for a few days of fishing. So, when I called him to ask if he would like to go to Canada with Elmer, my fishing buddy Lou, my son Jeff and me, I was not surprised at his reply and enthusiasm. He immediately agreed to call and reserve his favorite cabin, the one with two bedrooms that could sleep six or eight. This one came with a well pump inside that emptied directly into the sink.

The day finally came when we were to leave for the trip to Canada. We left Hershey in the late afternoon, drove two hours to pick up my father and then headed for the lake in Canada, another twelve hours away. The overnight drive was uneventful and the next morning we found ourselves in a restaurant only a few miles from the lake. After breakfast, we stopped at the grocery store to stock up on food and then at the bait store to purchase fishing licenses. When all such stops were done, we headed out the dirt road to the inlet to the lake where we would spend the week.

By the time we got the car unloaded, all we wanted to do was grab a few hours of sleep. All except Elmer who declared, "Nope, let's go fishing – I need to catch a northern bigger than any of the ones Joe caught." My dad volunteered to take Elmer out fishing since Lou and I had done all of the driving on the trip up. Since Jeff had slept during most of the trip, he too was anxious to go fishing. So, they got our boat from the owner of the site and off they went while Lou and I headed to our beds for some much needed sleep. It seemed like only a few minutes had passed before they returned but, in actuality, several hours had gone by. They had two nice sized bass and some yellow perch that Elmer insisted on keeping but, no northern pike.

Later, when my dad caught me alone at the dock, he commented, "That Elmer is too impatient to catch fish. All he wants to do is run back and forth across the lake!" "And, he is forever getting his line snagged or tangled and in need of help." "Yep, I know," I answered. "I'll take him out for the rest of the week so you can get some decent fishing done," "We'll both take turns going out with him so we both get a chance to catch a few fish," was his reply.

As the week wore on, Elmer became more and more discouraged. The biggest northern pike anyone had caught measured only thirty-two inches. "Nope, won't do," Elmer kept saying. "Joe caught one forty-two inches and we have to best that." Well, as fate would have it, we didn't best that. And, by the end of the week, Elmer was getting on everyone's nerves. My dad who was usually a patient, docile man, even said to me, "I love that Elmer dearly but, I don't ever want to go on another fishing trip with him!" Jeff was having the best time of anyone on the trip. He had discovered that the groundhog living in the burrow just off the front porch was quite tame and would even come out when he whistled and eat out of his hand. During the week, that groundhog consumed all our salad fixings.

The solution to Elmer's problem turned out to be quite simple. I took his thirty-two inch northern and hung it from a tree limb. I then had Elmer stand several feet behind it and hold his right arm up in the air. When I used a little triangulation with the camera and some proper alignment of Elmer and the fish, the picture appeared to show Elmer holding up a fish of at least 50 inches long. I took several pictures to make sure I got a good one. When Elmer saw the pictures he could not believe how big the fish looked. "I never saw anything like that afore," he said excitedly. "Just wait until Joe sees the northern pike I caught in Canada!" Then, after a little thought, he said, "It spites me to have to lie to Joe and tell him I caught a fifty inch northern." His dilemma was solved when we suggested that he wouldn't be lying if he simply showed the picture to Joe and told him, "This is a picture of me and the biggest northern I caught while in Canada," without mentioning any size.

Not long after we returned home, Elmer called me to tell me that Joe had come over to see how he had done fishing. Elmer said, "I showed the picture to Joe and told him, "this is a picture of me and the biggest northern I caught up in Canada."" He then said that Joe's comment was, "Oh my word, I never caught one that big up there! Next year you and me will go up and you can show me how and where to catch fish that big!"

Elmer, Ben and Me

I HAVE ALWAYS BEEN A dog lover, probably because I was always allowed to have one as a kid. At the time that we started building our house, we had a miniature poodle, named GiGi. GiGi was a great little dog, quiet, peaceful, totally devoted to our two sons and to Carole. GiGi was never a problem at all. But, GiGi was Carole's dog and GiGi wasn't much of a man's dog. I had been hunting since I was twelve years old and for the longest time, I had dreamed of the thrill and pleasure of hunting pheasant with a good bird dog by my side. An English setter, a man's dog; one who's ears could be scratched without getting out of the rocking chair by the fireplace. The reassurance of having a BIG dog curled up next to your feet on a cold winter's night. Yeah, that was going to be the kind of dog for me. And, we were finally building our dream house in the country, on a two-acre lot that would have plenty of room for a BIG dog to run.

One day, about that time, I was talking to a veterinary friend who was telling me about his hunting adventures with Molly, his English setter. "Yeah," Bud said, "there are three things in life that a man needs for real contentment – a four-wheeled drive vehicle, a boat and a good bird dog." "Yeah," I said, I don't have the boat or the four-wheeled drive vehicle yet, but I sure have spent a lot of time thinking about getting a good bird dog." "Well, I have three of Molly's puppies yet to sell," said Bud. That did it. I just had to see those puppies! I made arrangements to follow Bud home after work and look at his puppies. The first puppy to greet me when I entered Bud's house was a little, black-faced bundle of fur that was all over me with kisses all over my face and nips of my ears. And, oh that wonderful puppy-breath! I was hooked! I couldn't leave there without that little guy. Within minutes, I had whipped a check out of my wallet and that little guy was mine! On the drive home, he alternated between whining, trying to lick my face some more and sleeping. As I looked at him, I said, "What will we call you?" "You look like a 'Ben' to me." "That's who you will be, 'Ben'."

The closer I got to home, the more I began to wonder how Carole was going to take my bringing home a puppy without even asking if that would be okay with her. I pulled into the driveway, a little apprehensive about what her response would be. I walked into the house with Ben in my arms and handed him to her. "Meet Ben," I said as I thrust him into her arms. "What in the world did you go and do?" she asked. By then, Ben was licking her face and wagging his tail to-beat-the-band. "Oh, he is so cute," she said. "And, I just love puppy-breath." "What will we call him?" "His name is Ben," I said. "Ben?" "What kind of a name is that for a dog?" "I'm sorry, it is a good name and I have already named him." "What's for supper?" So, Ben became a part of our family!

Having had GiGi for about a dozen years, in no way prepared us for Ben. What a hand full he was! Typical field dog with an over abundance of energy! Ben could run for hours until he got so exhausted he would flop. And, run he did. There were many nights when I was out scouring the neighborhood looking for Ben. Someone would let him out and, away he would go. He was a natural born hunter. The thing that Ben didn't appreciate was that he was supposed to hunt with me! On nights when he would take off, Carole would say, "Well, we're not going to bed until he is safely in the house." So, I would be out running all over the neighborhood looking for him. Often I would come back at 2:00 AM, tired and dejected at having to tell Carole that I had failed to find Ben. Typically, she would say, "Oh, he came back an hour ago. He's upstairs in bed with the boys!"

I was an absolute failure at training Ben to be a bird dog! Actually, you don't train English Setters to be bird dogs, that is what they are and they take to bird hunting like ducks take to water. What I really failed at was training Ben to be a hunting dog. My hunting dog! One that would stick by my side, go on point and show me where the pheasants were hiding. Old Ben, he was like a greyhound out of the chute as soon as I took the leash off him. Zoom! Ben felt that he had to cover Elmer's entire farm in sixty seconds! I would stand in frustration watching pheasant rising into the air all over the farm! But, none of them ever close enough to be in my shooting range.

One day, just before the opening of pheasant season, I was talking with Elmer and he asked me how Ben was coming. He grinned as he said "Lizzie and me enjoy sitting on the porch in the evenings and watching pheasants fly into the air all over the farm!" "Elmer, I just don't know how to break him of that habit," I admitted. "Well, you know, I once had a hunting dog that did the same thing." "He wouldn't stick with me out in the field for anything." "How did you break him of that habit?" I asked. "Well, I tied a ten foot rope to his collar and tied the other end to a cinder block. That sure tired him out in a hurry and calmed him down so he would stick with me." Do you think that would work with Ben?" I asked. "Wouldn't hurt to try," he said. "The sooner you get him a little tired, the sooner he'll stick with you." That was it, the solution to my problem!

The next morning, my sons and I were eagerly anticipating the opening of pheasant season. We had the ideal situation, all we had to do was walk across the road and we had Elmer's entire farm as our own private hunting ground. I asked my son Scott to keep Ben on the leash until we were ready to begin. When I walked out of the garage carrying a cinder block, Scott asked me what in the world I intended to do with it. "You'll see," I said. "Today, Ben is going to hunt with us!" We walked across the road. Several days earlier, Elmer had plowed the field beside the cornfield. "This is perfect," I said. I tied one end of the rope to Ben's collar and the other end to the block. "Dad, that's not going to work!" said Jeff. "You'll see," I said. Well, by now Ben had reached his full size and he weighed about 85 pounds. He was a huge English setter! I set the block down on the ground and told Scott to take the leash off Ben. "Go get em, Ben. Fetch em out," I said. Zoom! Ben was off in a flash! He didn't even realize that he had a cinder block tied to him! He went racing off across that plowed field straight for the cornfield. That cinder block was a hitting the plowed furrows and bouncing into the air behind Ben, but he didn't even realize that it was there as he bounded into the corn. Suddenly, pheasants started taking to the air and heading for the boundaries of the farm. All around the farm, guns started going off as other hunters were treated to the spectacle of pheasants coming their way. For a short time, it sounded like Gettysburg! Scott and Jeff were doubled over in laughter!

We finally caught up to Ben on the far side of Elmer's cornfield. He was exhausted! Not only was he towing around that cinder block, he had been dragging an additional thirty pound or so of corn stalks that had ripped out of the ground and gotten tangled around the cinder block. We untied the cinder block and attached the leash. Ben, he just looked at us as if to say, "Boy, that was fun!" That night we ate meatloaf! The next day I drove over to Elmer's. "Elmer, what type of hunting dog was it that you tied that cinder block to?" I asked. "A beagle," was his reply!

Elmer and the Mountain

Next to fishing, Elmer liked deer hunting the best. Or, at least he thoroughly enjoyed going up to the cabin in deer season! There was one particular year when he couldn't make it up for opening day but said that if I drew up some directions, he could have his grandson, Darren, drive him up. Lou and I went up to the cabin on Saturday to kick back and relax over the weekend and hunt on Monday, the opening day. Neither of us saw anything with antlers on the opening day and, we were taking bets on whether or not Elmer would be able to find his way to the cabin. Sometime around 2:00 in the afternoon on the second day we came back to the cabin, again empty handed to find Elmer's old Plymouth parked beside the cabin. Two hours later Elmer and Darren were at the door. "Did you see anything when you were out?" Elmer asked. "Nope, all we have seen were does. Nothing with horns." Was our reply. "They're all up on top," said Elmer. "What do you mean by top?" I asked. "You know, the whole way to the top. Me and Darren just came from there and there's plenty of sign up on top. That's where they are," he said. "Are you sure you were the whole way to the top?" I asked. "Yep, we were and that's where they are. If we go to the top tomorrow, we are sure to get one," he said excitedly.

Several million years ago, or whenever the mountain behind the cabin was being formed, it pushed up. And, then, the very top pushed up a whole lot more. The result was that the mountain behind the cabin rises gradually for about ¾ of the way to the top and then the last quarter goes almost straight up.

The next morning we were up before first light, eagerly anticipating our trek to the top of the mountain. After breakfast we headed out. By the time we reached the ¾ mark we were all huffing and puffing. "Elmer, are you sure you and Darren were to the top of that?" I asked as I pointed up. "Well, we must have come up a different way cause it wasn't quite that steep yesterday. But, I'm sure we were to the top. That's where they are," he said. "OK" was my reply. I suggested that Lou and Darren hunt off to the right until they found an easier way to the top. Elmer and I would do the same going to the left. Once on top, Lou and Darren would stay in place and Elmer and I would hunt toward them. That way, if there were any deer on top, we would push them out to Lou and Darren. They departed, headed to the right and Elmer and I headed left.

Now, Elmer and I differ in our approach to hunting just like we do in fishing. I like to go through the woods slow, quiet and careful while Elmer sort of imitates a roadrunner. So, it didn't take more than a few minutes for me to spot him way out ahead of me. I didn't want to yell to him and frighten away any deer that might be in the woods so I figured that once he found an easier way up the mountain he would wait until I caught up or come back for me.

After about a mile I still hadn't seen Elmer again nor had I found an easier way up to the top. "I must have missed him or the place where he went up the mountain," I said to myself. "Oh well, I guess there is nothing else to do except bite the bullet and make my way to the top." I removed the bullets from my gun and slung the gun over my back so I would have both hands free in climbing. Up I went, climbing from one boulder to the next. By the time I got near the top I had unzipped my hunting coat and unbuttoned my flannel shirt. I was huffing like crazy and sweating up a storm. It was just about then that a gust of wind swept the hat from my head. The last I saw of it - it was disappearing out of sight waaaaay below me. I didn't know whether to go on up or to turn around and go back down. A quick look at my back-trail convinced me I would continue going up. Hopefully, once I reached the top, Lou and Darren could show me an easier way down. Eventually, I crawled over the last boulder and lay panting and gasping for breath. When I finally got around to looking up, there were three hunters about a hundred feet away just looking at me. In fact, in every direction that I looked I saw fluorescent orange hunting gear. There had to be more hunters than deer on that mountaintop! Finally, one of the three walked over and asked me where I came from. "I just climbed up from below," was my reply. "Why didn't you just drive up?" he asked. "The road is only a half-mile that way and it's an easy, level walk in from the parking spaces along the road!"

Thanking him for the information and vowing that I would never again climb that mountain, I started out in search of Lou and Darren. But, I never did find them. Neither did I find a way down that was any easier than the climb up. At last, I bit the bullet once again and climbed down to the base of the peak. When I got down, Lou, Darren and Elmer were waiting for me. "We could see you while you were climbing down," Lou said. "How did you get up there?" "I climbed up looking for Elmer," was my reply. Elmer just stood there staring up at the top. Finally he muttered, "A guy would have to be plumb crazy to climb up there. Why you could git a heart attack doing that!"

The Big Bobber

Every year, at about the time that the forsythia bloom, the tree peepers begin their mating cacophonies and the trout lilies and skunk cabbage start to poke their tips through the ground, trout season opens in Pennsylvania. Opening day is typically the middle Saturday in April. And, every year, beginning in March, Elmer would begin asking me when I was going to take him fishing.

While I have never considered myself a fly fishing purist, it has always been my favorite method of fishing. There is just something about the skill, concentration, stealth, and delicacy of presentation that is necessary to imitate nature and fool those wary trout that makes this sport especially appealing to me. I have always reveled in the ability to immerse myself into the natural surroundings in a fashion that is only possible when you are alone on a stream. The ability to close your eyes and allow your other senses to come alive is a special treat. The babbling of a brook, the sounds of a trout sipping nymphs, the hum of an insect hatch, the gentle flapping of a bird's feathers against the air, the slightly cooler and more refreshing breeze above the water or the smell of mountain laurel in bloom never fail to put me into a euphoric mood. These are the things that cleanse the soul, reemphasize the really important things in life and reaffirm that everything is all right in the world.

Elmer was not a fly fisherman. Elmer preferred a spinning rod rigged with a large bobber (tennis ball sized) and a night crawler. He needed to be able to see rather than sense when a fish was biting. There was nothing delicate about his rod; it was a one-size- fits-all type. Elmer felt that if it was heavy enough to use for ten-pound carp or catfish, it certainly ought to be able to handle a one-pound trout! Waders or hip boots were not for Elmer. When he went fishing, he preferred his thigh-high barn boots. Therefore, wading, while fishing, was out of the question for him. He needed a nice spot on the bank where he could sit and fish. While I loved him dearly, his fishing style and mine were totally at odds. As such, I normally got him settled into a good fishing hole and then I went up or down stream so I could fish the way I wanted to fish.

On one particular Sunday morning, we had gone early to Stony Creek. Stony Creek is a pristine, freestone mountain stream that runs from east to west through the mountains just north of Harrisburg, PA before emptying into the Susquehanna River. Its waters are crystal clear with each pool lower than the one before and connected by riffles or tiny waterfalls that burble over and around boulders. After making sure that Elmer was all set with plenty of hooks, sinkers and worms, I left him to mosey downstream in search of my own pool. I walked the bank, not an easy task as the banks are heavily lined with Mountain Laurel, our wild rhododendrons, in search of an ideal spot to fish. About a hundred yards downstream, I came to a relatively long pool that was fairly deep at its head end and got gradually shallower as it flowed toward the riffles at its tail end. Just before the riffles, it flowed against an undercut bank. As I scanned the pool, my attention was caught by a large trout of at least 16 inches that was holding in the calmer and shadowed waters just under the undercut bank on the far side. Watching through an opening in the laurel I could see the trout move about a foot out from its feeding lie every time a caddis or mayfly drifted by on the surface. The trout would edge over, in direct line with the floating insect, gently rise, suck it in and return to the sanctity of the shadow under the bank. Most of the water between me and the trout was no more than a foot or so deep. To get into position to cast my fly without spooking the trout was going to be difficult. My first cast had to be perfect and I probably wouldn't get a second one without scaring the trout into deeper water.

I moved downstream so as to be out of the trout's line of sight. Extreme stealth was necessary in order to get far enough out into the stream to have space for a back-cast that would allow the line and especially the fly to be laid gently on the water, above the trout, so that it would drift like a natural insect. Any slight mistake would spook the trout. Ripples in the water from my wading or anything less than a perfect cast and it would all be over. I spent the next fifteen minutes inching my way out into the stream. After what seemed like hours I had arrived at the perfect spot for the cast and, the trout was still feeding. With my heart racing and my adrenalin pumping, I began to slowly unreel the right amount of line in preparation for the cast. Just then there came a horrendous crashing in the underbrush across the stream from me. The crashing was followed by some muffled epithets and the popping of Elmer out through the foliage. He had tripped over a root, his pants were torn at the knee and his knee was bleeding. He looked up, spotted me and shouted, "Hey Ken, is that you? Are you ketchin enny?" Before I could even reply, there was a WHIZZZZ as his bobber came arching out over the stream. It went kersplat! in the water about six feet upstream from MY trout. My whole body sagged as I looked for the trout to go speeding for cover. Instead of heading for cover, it went flying upstream like a miniature version of a dolphin. I had never seen anything like it! That trout attacked Elmer's night crawler like it hadn't eaten in weeks! As the bobber disappeared beneath the water, Elmer let out a "whoop!" and set the hook.

All the way home I was treated to "Hee, hee, hee. Well, Ken, you caught the most, but I caught the biggest one. Boy, I can't wait to show this one to Lizzie!"

Elmer and the Environmental Samples

Some months after the accident at Three Mile Island (TMI), a series of emergency drills were scheduled to test everyone's capabilities and to help train those who needed such training. For one such drill, I was invited to participate as an independent observer. I readily accepted the invitation thinking that this would be a way to help and feeling confident that it would be a learning experience.

On the designated day, I went early to the office of the Bureau of Radiation Protection to receive my assignment. I was assigned to a field team that included Jim and Jane. We were to go out to a pre-determined location and take periodic radiation readings and relay them back to our team leader, Maggie.

Initially, this adventure was fun. We drove to our assigned location, on a hill overlooking TMI. Once there, we rechecked our clipboards, spread sheets and radiation detectors and prepared to fulfill our part of the exercise. Although the radiation readings that we took were all just normal background readings, the numbers phoned in gradually increased according to the preplanned scenario. As the day wore on, the whole process became increasingly boring and routine. The temperature slowly rose into the high 80s and every time we went out to take a reading the black flies and gnats would attack with abandon. Fortunately, our car had air conditioning that allowed us to keep the windows closed by occasionally running the engine and letting the air conditioner keep the car tolerably cool. By noon the tedium was affecting us and we were sounding like a bunch of little kids headed on vacation with many "Isn't this thing over yet?"

Finally, around 3:00 in the afternoon, we were given the order to abandon site, pick up some environmental samples and head on in. Jim, Jane and I looked at each other and asked the same question, "What kind of environmental samples do we collect?" After several minutes of such discussion, I suggested we drive over to Elmer's farm and collect our samples so that we wouldn't frighten anyone who saw us doing it.

When we pulled into Elmer's yard, we found him pulling weeds in Lizzie's garden. He welcomed us heartily since we gave him the perfect excuse to take a break from his assigned chore. I introduced Jim and Jane and told him what we were doing. "Yep, I know. When that accident was going on they came by and told me that I might have to evacuate. I told them, "Don't be crazy. I've got steers to feed and I don't believe that what you say is gonna happen." "I told them that if they just left them engineers alone, they would get that thing under control. Them engineers, they know what they are doing." "Hey, wanna come inside and see my arryhead collection?"

We gently declined his offer and explained that we were pressed for time to collect our environmental samples and get them back to the labs. Elmer got one of his impish looks on his face and suggested that there were a lot of environmental samples in his meadow. "A guy who used to live here called them samples 'poor boy Frisbees'."

We went through the gate and out into his meadow. It was indeed full of those "poor boy frisbees." We found them in various stages of dryness from very moist, olive green ones to dry, tan ones. When we got to where we could see up around the bend, we discovered the source. Elmer had about forty young steers grazing in the meadow. "What do you think?" I asked. "Should we take some of these samples to Maggie?" Jim readily agreed but Jane wavered. She wasn't sure if Maggie would appreciate our sense of humor. But, we finally talked her into it. It didn't take very long to fill half a garbage bag with the dry ones.

When we got back to the car, Elmer was there to meet us and tell us that we just had to come up on the porch and have some of the iced tea that Lizzie had made for us. We followed him up to the porch and, we were treated to some delicious iced tea made from the fresh mint from Lizzie's garden. "While you're this close, you might as well come on in and see my arryhead collection, "Elmer said. With no way to escape, we dutifully followed him into the house and let him tell us his story about each arrowhead that was found on the farm.

As soon as we could gracefully excuse ourselves, we thanked Elmer and Lizzie for their hospitality, promised to return when we had more time and headed back to the office. Several times on the drive back, Jane expressed her reservations about what we were about to do. "You're going to get me into trouble with my boss," she said. As it turned out, Jane's apprehension was unfounded. In her typical undaunted fashion, Maggie opened the bag and exclaimed, "Oh goody, we get to measure the pasture-to-milk pathway!" "Okay, get them down to the lab for immediate analysis." As we turned toward the door, she said, "You guys did good today. You all get A's."

For some reason, unbeknownst to me, I was never invited to participate in another drill!

Elmer and the Air Raid Siren

When the Accident at Three Mile Island occurred, my friend, Bill moved into the area to help out at the Island and to take part in the recovery. He needed a place to stay and called me to ask if I knew of any place that he might rent. I told him that my neighbor, Elmer, had told me earlier in the week that he was looking for someone to rent half of his farmhouse. For Bill, that would be perfect. He had grown up on a farm. Two days later, he moved into half of Elmer's farmhouse.

Bill and Elmer hit it off from the very start. Due in part to Bill's familiarity with farm life but more importantly to the fact that Bill had grown up only a stone's throw from Black Lake in New York. Every time I saw Elmer after that he would tell me that Bill wanted us to go to Black Lake fishing with him. Well, Lou, Bill, Elmer and I finally did go on that fishing trip to Black Lake and, we caught a lot of fish.

Long after Bill moved on to another job, Elmer kept asking me, "When are you going to take me to Black Lake fishing?" My reply was always the same, "Yeah, we'll go up sometime." Over the next summer he brought up the subject so many times that I finally told him that I would make arrangements and we would go. I figured that it was the only way that I could stop him from asking me about it. When I called up about a cabin, at a place of Elmer's choosing, the first opening was in September, after Labor Day. So, I booked a cabin for a week. For the rest of the summer, I was continually chauffeuring Elmer to various stores so he could get more bobbers or more hooks or more of whatever fishing lure someone had told him about.

The day finally came when we were to leave for Black Lake. I wasn't really anticipating the drive because Black Lake is way up at the top of New York and it takes nine hours to drive up there from home. But, I had a new station wagon and was at least anticipating the chance to see how it did on a long drive. Besides, I always get at least a little excited about the chance to go fishing. When I pulled into Elmer's yard he met me at the car and said, "Well, I have it all loaded and gassed up and ready to go." "What are you talking about?" I asked him. "My car," he said. "Elmer, we're going to take my car; it's brand new," I said. "Nope, you always use your car and it's not right. This time we will take mine; Lizzie washed it for us," he said. We argued, but Elmer was not one to give in when he had his mind set on something. I really didn't want to take his car since it was a fifteen year-old Plymouth that had a hole in the seat on the driver's side and a trunk that was full of fine dust from all the trips it had made in and out his dirt lane. When he told me that Lizzie had put a cushion on the front seat so I wouldn't have to sit in the hole, what more could I say? Off we went. The trip passed without incident and we arrived at Black Lake just before dark. Our cabin was one of four, sitting on a bluff about twenty feet above the lake. It didn't have any kind of heating system, but it did have a gas-fired refrigerator, gas range top and a well pump (the old fashioned type) that pumped directly into the sink. The lake was our only bathtub and the outhouse was at the end of the path.

We turned in early that night because it had been a long and tiring trip and because we were going fishing early because that was when Elmer said they were biting best. I have always been one of those who sleeps the sleep of the dead. I think that it is called "REM" sleep. At any rate, once my head hits the pillow, I am out for the night. Somewhere around 3:00 AM I found myself in the streets of Paris with bombs going off all around me, buildings disintegrating from the explosions and air raid sirens blaring. Those blessed sires, why won't they stop? Ever so slowly I began the climb upward from sub-consciousness to reality. Finally, I was able to shake my head and open my eyes. But, no matter what I did, I couldn't make the sirens stop. Finally, I called to Elmer, "Elmer, what is that noise?" "I don't know, it is coming from across the lake," was his reply. After listening for a few seconds more, I declared, "No, Elmer, it is right outside our door!" I jumped up, ran to the door and cracked it open. The noise was coming from Elmer's car! It was his horn! I ran out, opened the car door and banged on the horn. Nothing, it kept blowing. What am I to do? It finally dawned on me that if I pull the battery cable, it would stop. I ran back inside and got the pliers out of my tackle box. Elmer was snoring. Back out, I threw up the hood, loosened the bolt on the battery terminal and twisted it off the battery. At last, blissful silence! As I gently let the hood back down I glanced at the ground and could see my footprints all around. There was a heavy frost on the ground. That is why I was I shivering so! At that instant, I remembered that I always sleep in the buff and I had not stopped to put anything on. Thankfully, we were the only ones in the cabins that night. I ran into the cabin, shivering. Elmer was still snoring. I crawled back into my bed but the shivering wouldn't stop and sleep wouldn't come. At 5:00 AM Elmer popped out of bed to declare, "Hey Ken, are you going to sleep all day? It's time to go fishing!"

Hunting Lessons from Elmer

Elmer loved to fish and Elmer loved to hunt. And, Elmer loved to have me take him fishing and hunting. Unfortunately, Elmer required a lot of attention whenever he did either. When I took him fishing, I usually spent all my time getting him unhooked from the bushes that he seemed to prefer casting into rather than the water. And, he was forever losing tackle and in need of assistance to re-rig his rod so he could resume fishing. When it came to tackle, he never seemed to have the right stuff. His hooks were gigantic in size, more suitable for shark fishing than for trout or bass. His bobbers, which he insisted on using no matter what type of fishing he was doing, were tennis ball sized. They were not the sort of thing you wanted on your line when stealth was indicated so as not to scare the fish. If we were using a boat, according to Elmer, we were never in the right spot and so, he kept insisting that we move. "We need to go over to the other side where those two boats are, that's where they are biting." The end result was that boat fishing with Elmer was equivalent to running the boat back and forth across the lake or the river. Part of this, I came to realize, was due to the fact that Elmer just couldn't remain still for any length of time at all.

When we were hunting for deer, Elmer was the same way. He could not bring himself to sit in the woods and wait for the deer to come to him. Rather, he felt that he could go to the deer. The result was that he was constantly on the move while in the woods hunting for deer. Now, this is exactly the opposite of the way I grew up learning to hunt for deer. Even when I was just starting out as a twelve year old, I quickly came to the conclusion that most hunters in the woods were just like Elmer. They were constantly on the move. As a result, they were constantly chasing but seldom seeing the deer. I learned that I could be very successful at deer hunting by going slowly and quietly through the woods and stopping every few steps to study the woods around me. By doing so, I bagged a deer nearly every year I hunted simply by letting all the other hunters chase the deer to me.

One year Elmer and I went up to my cabin to hunt deer. The land on the mountain above my cabin is owned by a man who invites a number of his friends and relatives to hunt with him during the first week. So, although I have his permission to hunt on his property, I usually avoid going up on the mountain until the second week. Instead, I go below the cabin where the hunting pressure is considerably less than it is above the cabin. If not below the cabin, I drive up Cherry Run Road and hunt on top of the mountain in the State Forrest lands. On this one particular year, when Elmer went with me I decided to start out by going below the cabin. Elmer and I walked down to the area together but as soon as we started into the woods, he quickly outpaced me and, the last time I looked, he was disappearing through the trees ahead of me. I walked only a short distance into the woods when I noticed a colossal hemlock tree that had apparently escaped the axes of a century earlier when such trees were being decimated for their bark that was needed for the leather tanning industry. That old tree had lower branches that must have been a good thirty feet long. Where the lower ones connected to the tree, they were about six feet off the ground and their tips were about three feet off the ground. I decided that this would make a good place to sit and watch for deer. So, I crawled back into the dimness under the limbs and sat with my back against the trunk of the tree. From this vantage point, I was pretty much hidden from view but had an excellent view of the woods all around me.

I could not have been sitting under the hemlock tree for more than a few minutes when I caught a flicker in my peripheral vision to my left.

As I watched, a total of sixteen deer came through the woods and passed in front of me. However, none had horns and it was antlered season only. In no more than a few minutes after the deer had gone on through the woods, I spotted additional movement to my left. This happened to be Elmer who was headed in the same direction as the deer. I stayed put and didn't say anything as Elmer walked on past and disappeared into the woods on my right.

About an hour later, I detected motion on my right. As I watched, a total of eighteen deer came through the woods and passed below me. A few minutes later, Elmer came from the same direction and again passed by me without seeing me. A half hour or so later, the whole process was repeated. It was amazing how all those deer kept passing by me without ever sensing that I was there watching them. It was also amazing that Elmer did the same thing.

In yet another hour the cycle repeated itself. However, this time, when I saw Elmer coming, I decided that it was time to show myself and ask him why he kept chasing all those antler-less deer through the woods. I crawled out from under the tree and walked down to intercept his path. When he saw me, his comment was, "There's nothing down here. I haven't seen a deer all morning. They're up above your cabin, that's where all the shooting is. We need to go up there."

I didn't have the heart to tell Elmer that while he had seen no deer, he had chased a total of seventy past me. We went back to the cabin and ate a hurried lunch because Elmer was anxious to head up on the mountain where he was certain all the deer were. We spent the afternoon on the mountain where I saw an additional eleven deer but Elmer didn't see any. By the time we met up he was convinced that all the deer had run down the mountain to the woods below my cabin because, "That's where all the shooting is."

The Canada Goose

ELMER'S FARM IS APPARENTLY located along at least a minor flyway for Canada geese, snow geese and swans as they stop over on his farm by the thousands when the weather begins to break each year around the end of February. At one time, he also had about eight Canada geese that stayed on his farm all the time. Primarily, they stayed because the grand patriarch of the clan was a goose with a crippled wing. The problem with the wing prevented him from flying more that a hundred yards or so at a time. The remainder of the group that stayed were obviously offspring from this one old guy and his mate as they were always together as a group. Elmer, like many farmers steadily received requests from hunters for permission to hunt on his farm. Most of these requests he denied. However, a few learned that Elmer was a sucker for a hard-luck tale. They would stop by, talk to him for a while and tell him that they were out of work and that sure made it hard to keep their families fed. So, when they asked if he minded if they came and hunted a day or two on his farm, he usually relented.

One fall, Elmer and I were talking when he mentioned that unusually large numbers of geese had been stopping over. He said that they were getting to be such a pest that he figured he would have to shoot a few and stick them in his freezer to discourage so many from stopping over. Well, I had grown up on wild game and so when he told me that he was going to shoot a few, I told him that if he got an extra one, I would like to give wild goose a try. He promised that he would get me one. Around the middle of November, Elmer stopped over one evening and gave me a plastic wrapped package. "What's this?" I asked. "Well, you said you wanted me to get you a Canada goose, so, I got you one. And, Lizzie cleaned it for you" he said. "That's great. You know what, I'm going to stick this in the freezer and surprise the family with it for Christmas dinner. Thank you and thank Lizzie for me too," I said.

A day or two before Christmas, I got the goose out of the freezer so it would thaw out in time for roasting on Christmas day. We were going to have an old fashioned Christmas dinner – one like our forefathers enjoyed!

Christmas morning came and Carole made the stuffing, I stuffed the goose and together we put it in the oven, figuring on having Christmas dinner around 2:00 in the afternoon. Two o'clock came but the goose wasn't any where near being ready to come out of the oven. I couldn't even get a fork to penetrate it. "Better give it a while longer," I told Carole. Meanwhile, everyone was getting hungry. So, we made sandwiches to tide everyone over. At 4:00 we again tested the bird and found that nothing had changed. "We better turn the oven temperature up," Carole said. So, we did. An hour later, everyone was asking, "When are we going to eat?" By 6:00 the situation with the goose hadn't improved – that bird was still as tough as an old work boot! "Sorry, everyone. I didn't realize that wild geese took so long to cook," I said. By 7:00 everyone was famished and the goose still wasn't done. Fortunately, we found a Chinese take-out place that was open. That Christmas, our dinner consisted of Chinese food with pumpkin pie for desert. At bedtime, the goose was still too tough to take out of the oven. I told Carole to go to bed and that I would stay up until the goose was done. The next morning she found me asleep on the sofa but the goose still wasn't done. "This thing is never going to get done," she said. "Well, we're just going to keep cooking it until it is," was my reply. At 4:00 o'clock that afternoon, I finally agreed with Carole that it was a hopeless cause and we resigned the goose to the garbage can. Several days later, Elmer stopped by to ask how we enjoyed the Christmas goose. I felt bad having to tell him "I'm sorry, Elmer but, that bird must have been a hundred years old!" "No matter how long we cooked it, and we cooked it for twenty-eight hours, it never got tender enough to stick a fork in it." "I wouldn't doubt it," was his only reply.

Several months went by and one Sunday afternoon I decided to walk over and fish for bass in Elmer's pond. As usual, I wasn't there for more than fifteen minutes when I noticed him out by his barn digging worms. He soon joined me at the pond with his fishing rod, bobber and can of worms. We fished for a little while and then our moving around the pond in opposite directions finally brought us together. "Elmer, I don't see your flock of Canada geese anywhere," I said. "Nope, they're all gone," he said. "Well, how can that be?" I asked. "That old gander couldn't fly?' I said. "Nope, he ain't here no more," said Elmer. "Why, what happened?" I asked. "Well, one of those guys that I left hunt on the farm last fall came to the house and said he shot a goose that flew over him at the back end of the farm and it came down in the pond. He said he was pretty sure it was dead and wanted to know if he could go down and get it out of the pond. "I told him, OK, but don't do any shooting down at the pond." "Well, he wasn't gone more than five minutes when Lizzie and me heard him shooting down at the pond. I came down and told him to get off the farm. He told me that his goose was floating in the pond and I told him to leave it and go. After he left, I fished the goose out of the pond and, you know what, it was that old one with the crippled wing. He shot it right here on the pond!" "Aw, no, that's terrible!" I said. "What did you do with the goose?" I asked. "Oh, I fished it out of the pond and took it up to Lizzie. She cleaned it for a good neighbor for Christmas dinner!" he said. I walked home thinking that I was so glad that that goose never got tender enough for us to eat!

A Ferhoodled Elmer

When we first moved to Hershey, it was a sleepy little country town with a population of approximately fourteen thousand. The surrounding areas were pretty much all dairy farms and there were only two traffic lights between my home in the country and the Medical Center where I worked. On most days, I could make it from my home to the Medical Center parking lot in eight to ten minutes. This allowed me, whenever time or schedule permitted, to go home for lunch. These breaks from the routine were invigorating. They gave me a chance to have a quiet lunch with Carole and refresh my mindset to where I was eager to take on the problems of the afternoon with gusto.

On one particular spring day, I headed home all aglow because after several rainy and cloudy days, this particular day broke with a clear sky and a sunshine that had been anticipated all winter. It was a glorious day with the buds popping out on the trees, the perfume of the lilacs in the air and the birds scurrying to complete their nests. It was an ideal day – the kind of day that only comes along once or twice each year. I was in an elated frame of mind.

I pulled in the driveway, got out of my car and attempted to imitate the cacophony of bird songs that the mockingbird was serenading me with. I went into the house, hugged the dogs, hugged Carole and commented on what a grand and glorious day this one was. Carole and I had just sat down to have lunch when Carole said, "Elmer is walking up the driveway." I went outside and asked Elmer, "What are you doing, taking up hiking?" He looked at me and said, "I'm all ferhoodled." ("ferhoodled" is a Pennsylvania Dutch term for befuddled or messed up or extremely disorganized) I asked him, "Why, what is the matter?" He told me that he had been out spreading manure when his tractor "stayed stick." ("stayed stick" is another Pennsylvania Dutch saying for "got stuck") "How did you manage that?" I asked. He told me about how he was spreading manure when he came to a particularly wet looking area in his back field. He said that he should have gone around it but instead had attempted to drive through it and that is when his tractor "stayed stick."

"What do you plan to do about it?" I asked. "Well, I don't think it will take much to get it unstuck," was his reply. "We just need something to put under the wheel to give it some traction and it will come right out," he said. "What do you have in mind?" I asked. "If you have a board or a piece of plank, that should do," he said. "It won't take much," he added. I checked my garage and found a five-foot piece of 2 by 8. "That should do the trick," Elmer declared. So, we went hoofing it out to his back field. I let him carry the 2 by 8 because I was dressed in slacks, a white shirt and tie.

When we got to his tractor, I did not see any way a small piece of board was going to get him out of the rut he was in. It was obvious that he had spun the wheels and dug the rut deeper. Between the mud and manure mixed with water in the rut, it didn't look like anything short of another tractor or a tow truck would get him out. Elmer climbed up on the tractor and started it up. "Elmer, don't do anything until I get a look from behind," I told him. I walked back to the space between the tractor and the manure spreader and bent down to have a look. At that exact time, Elmer decided to pop the clutch and show me how the wheel spun without any traction. Well, the spinning tractor wheel threw at least 30 gallons of water liberally laced with mud and steer manure directly at me. I was hit from head to toe. "Oops," said Elmer. I would have said a few other things if I weren't so busy spitting out a mixture of mud and manure at the time. "Elmer, call one of your son-in-laws (he had two son-in-laws who lived on farms within a mile of his) and get them to come over and help you. I'm going home to take a shower," I said as I stormed off trying to pull mud out of my hair.

Carole saw me coming up the driveway and met me at the door. She was doubled over in laughter with tears streaming down her cheeks as she told me to go into the garage and strip before even thinking about coming into the house. "And, put your clothes in one of the garbage cans," she added. As I turned and headed for the garage, she said, "Phew, you stink!"

By the time I showered and scrubbed my skin till it glowed, I didn't have time to eat lunch before heading back to the office.

It might have been my imagination but I swear that everyone I talked to that afternoon was sniffing at me.

Snapper Soup

Snapper soup is a gastronomic delight, especially when the bowls of it are liberally sprinkled with sherry just before serving. The best snapper soup is made using the meat of the snapping turtle, *Chelydra serpentina serpentine*. When you see a live snapping turtle, the last thing you think about is eating it! They are ugly, they are vicious when threatened, they are usually covered with mud from the pond bottoms they call home and they are a throwback to the dinosaur period with their armor-plated carapaces and saw-edged tails. Their powerful beak-like jaws add to their ferocious look and, I have often heard, but never experienced, that they can bite through a broom handle. As kids, we hunted them every spring as they were a welcome addition to our food supply.

The process of preparing a snapping turtle for the kettle first involves several dunks into scalding water to remove the outer skin, carapace plates and toe nails. The cleaned shell is usually kept and added to the soup where it dissolves and acts as a thickener for the soup. It is said that President William Howard Taft was so fond of turtle soup that he brought a special chef into the White House to specifically make it for him.

One summer evening, Elmer called me and asked me to come over. When I drove up, I found him and Lizzie sitting on the front porch. Elmer told me that he had a problem. "What's that?" I asked. "There's a big old snapping turtle down there in the pond that we need to get out or it is going to eat all of Lizzie's little ducks." "No kidding!" was my reply. "Yep, me and Lizzie been sitting here watching the baby ducks disappear one at a time. They will be swimming around and, all of a sudden just disappear with nothing left where they were but a few bubbles. That's a big old snapping turtle that does that," he explained. "What do you want me to do about it?" I asked. "Tell Jeff to come over and set out a trotline," Elmer explained. "He can catch him and the guy who owns the restaurant up the road will buy him for $2.00 a pound."

Jeff was my youngest son and he was about twelve years old at the time. He and his friend, Danny, were always looking for some way to get rich quick. So, when I told them what Elmer had proposed, they immediately called the owner of the local restaurant to verify that he would buy the snapper from them for $2.00 a pound. He told them that he would do that; so, they set off for the pond to string their trotline, baited with pieces of bluegills. As luck would have it, when they checked their trotline the next morning, they discovered that they had caught the snapping turtle. Elmer weighed it for them and it tipped the scales at just a hair over twenty pounds. The boys were excited and they came home carrying their catch in a five-gallon bucket that Elmer had loaned them. Since, at the moment, I was tied up with a project, Carole was tapped to serve as chauffer and drive the boys to the restaurant where they would collect their princely sum.

About 20 minutes after they left, the phone rang. It was Carole calling to tell me that the restaurant owner had reneged on his offer to the boys and instead of the $2.00 per pound, he was now telling them that he would give them, at the most, five dollars for the turtle. He said that when he made the offer, he didn't expect two boys their ages to be able to catch a snapping turtle. Carole asked me what she should do. I told her to bring the boys and the turtle back home and I would buy it from them. "What in the world are you going to do with it?" she asked. "I will make snapper soup," was my reply. "You do not know how to make snapper soup!" she said. "Oh, but I do," I assured her.

I figured that this would be a great opportunity to teach my son and my wife how to make snapper soup. However, as soon as the cleaning process began, Carole decided that there were some errands that required her immediate attention. As soon as we verified that the turtle did not contain eggs, Jeff and Danny lost interest and went off to plot all the wonderful things they were going to do with their newfound wealth. So, I was left on my own to make the soup without having anyone but the dogs to share my recipe with. That twenty pound snapping turtle made about two gallons of snapper soup; and, it was incredible! We thoroughly enjoyed it with dinner that evening and the next two evenings to follow. We even had enough to freeze and share with everyone who joined us for Thanksgiving dinner that fall. For Christmas, we had roasted duck compliments of Lizzie who cleaned two and sent them over to us in appreciation for saving her little duckling from almost certain annihilation by that snapping turtle.

Elmer and the Big Stringer

Every time I took Elmer on a fishing trip to Black Lake I came home and told Carole that I would never again go to Black Lake with Elmer. It seemed like every time we went up there, something incredibly frustrating happened. It was on one particular trip that I became convinced that motors hated me! In preparation for that trip, I took my outboard motor to the shop beforehand and had it tuned up so that I wouldn't have to spend my days rowing Elmer around the lake. Wouldn't you know it, once we got there that blasted motor would not start no matter what I did.

The morning after we arrived, Elmer had me up before sunrise, all eager to go "catch some big ones." We hurried through breakfast and loaded the boat. Then, I sat in the boat pulling the starter cord on that engine until I got blisters on most of my fingers. No matter what I tried, it would not start. While I sat there getting more and more frustrated with the motor, Elmer was having a ball, standing up in the boat and casting his lures every which way. And, about every fourth cast he would get hung up. "Ken" he would say, "I did it again." And, each time, he expected me to stop what I was doing and row him over so he could get his lure unstuck. The experience was so frustrating that at one point I rowed to the middle of the lake, planning to throw the outboard engine overboard. Fortunately, or unfortunately, Elmer talked me out of doing that. I spent the next four days rowing him all over the lake.

After that trip I came home and told Carole, "That's it, I can't take it any more. I will never go to Black Lake with Elmer again." "We'll see" was her only reply.

Well, about the first of the next April, Elmer started asking me when we were going to go back up to Black Lake. Not wanting to hurt his feeling, I kept telling him that I didn't think that I would be able to make it this summer. "Oh, I'm sure you can find a few days. Right after I get through with the harvest will be best for me" was his ever reply. While I kept putting him off, his efforts to get me to go only intensified. Finally, near the end of August I again relented and called Lou to see if he wanted to go to Black Lake with Elmer and me. "As long as we rent a decent cabin – one with indoor plumbing and heat – and, we rent a boat with a motor that works" was his reply. So, I called a friend who went to Black Lake every year and got a phone number for the owners of the cabins he rented. I called and reserved a three bedroom cabin with indoor plumbing, oil heat and a full kitchen and a boat with a working motor. Hey, how could this trip be so bad – what with a cabin that provided all the comforts of home and a boat with a real working motor? I was even starting to anticipate the trip.

We arrived at the cabin on a chilly September evening with a drizzling rain coming down and the winds kicking up. Oh well, I had brought several books to read and we would wait it out – how bad could it be? Little did I realize just how bad it could be, stuck in a cabin with Elmer when he was just "busting at the seams to go fishing." It was impossible to read when he kept up a steady conversation about how it "looks like it is stopping – let's get our gear into the boat." About six times a day we carried our gear down to the boat only to have it start raining harder and forcing us to make a hasty retreat to the cabin. Every time Elmer would hear a boat on the lake, he would say, "Them other guys are going out – the rain must be stopping – let's go." AAARGH! How I grew to hate being stuck in a cabin with Elmer when it was raining and he wanted to go fishing!

On the third and last morning that we were there, the sun came up and while it was pretty windy, the sky was clear. "Let's go," Elmer said. "I can't go home without a mess of fish to take back to Lizzie." We weren't ten feet from shore when Elmer began casting and getting his lure hung up! After an hour we hadn't caught a thing. "Ken, you gotta find us some fish – I can't go home to Lizzie empty handed. That woman sure does like her fresh fish." I then remembered that the last time we came up in September, we caught most of our fish up at the end of the lake, where Black River comes into the lake. "Reel your rod in and hold on," I said. "I'll take you to some fish." It took about an hour to motor up the lake to the spot I had thought about. The trip, however, was well worth it as when we got there we found huge schools of large crappies and blue gills (Elmer's favorites). Lou and I were fishing with fly rods and rubber grubs. The fish went crazy for them! We were soon pulling fish in so fast that Elmer was spending all his time putting them on the stringer. "Boy, Oh boy, now we are getting a mess of good fish for Lizzie!" he clucked.

Unfortunately, after about an hour the clouds started rolling in, tadpole sized rain drops began falling and thunder started booming in the distance. "Pack it up – we have to make a run for it," I said. I started the engine and asked if everybody was ready to go. "Yes," was the dual reply. So, I open the throttle on the engine and started a hasty retreat back to the cabin. My hat blew off and into the lake but I wasn't about to stop or go back for it. It was getting cold. It was getting windy. My head was soaked and icy rain water was running down the inside of my collar. But, "It was worth it," I thought "to get Elmer his fish!" About half way down the lake, I looked back and, to my amazement, I saw fish floating on the lake. "What in the world is going on?" I thought. I stopped the boat and asked, "Elmer, Lou, where is the stringer of fish?" Elmer grabbed the stringer and lifted it into the air. All that remained was one single fish at the end of the stringer. All the while we were speeding down the lake, the stringer had been in the water and the fish had been coming off! Elmer was dumbfounded! "Quick," he shouted, "Let's go back and pick them up!" Well, I turned the boat around but by the time we got back to where I had seen any of the fish, they had disappeared beneath the surface. "What are we going to do?" Elmer cried. "That was the nicest stringer of fish I ever saw!" "How could you guys have left that happen?" "Elmer, hold tight. We're heading to the cabin to get out of this rain," was my only reply. "#@*&% dumbest thing I ever saw!" said Elmer, at least ten times on the way to the cabin. And, repeatedly after we got to the cabin. And, about every half hour on the ride home the next day! As we crossed from New York into Pennsylvania, my patience came to an end. After hearing "#@*&% dumbest thing I ever saw!" for the umpteenth time, I said, "Elmer, I can't take this any more – this will be my last trip to Black Lake." He was quiet for the rest of the drive home.

When I got home, I said to Carole, "That's the last trip that I will ever take to Black Lake with Elmer!" "We'll see" was her only reply.

Becoming an Auto Mechanic – Again

One of the many jobs I had as I struggled to work my way through college was working at a gas station. The year was 1961 and, it was not the modern kind of gas station but, the real kind; the kind where the attendant actually pumped the gas for the customer. And, while the gas was being pumped, the attendant washed the windshield and the rear window, checked the pressure in all four tires, verified the oil level and topped off the water in the battery. These are the sort of things that are not available today at even the so-called "Full Service" gas pumps. Sitting behind a counter and simply bar-scanning soda or snack purchases was, in those days, unheard of.

At least one weekend a month the price of regular gasoline was lowered from 19 cents to 15 cents per gallon and, with each fill-up the customer received two free water glasses or a coffee mug with a picture of Niagara Falls on it. Cars would be lined up all day waiting for a fill-up and the collection of their rewards. In addition to gas and oil, oil changes, lubes and tune-ups were also offered. Since the gas station was owned by the service center next door, the gas station also changed tires when things got backed up at the service center. Unfortunately, and all too often in those days the incentive offered for a gas tank fill-up was a free car wash.

While I didn't mind the routine things like pumping gas or changing tires I quickly developed a deep loathing for doing tune-ups and washing cars. I have always been a little klutzy when doing muscle-powered work in confined spaces. So, with almost every tune up or muffler change, a slipped wrench would result in a bleeding knuckle. To make matters worse, while doing tune-ups, you were still expected to take care of customers at the gas pumps. It seemed like every time I got heavily into a difficult job, someone would pull up for a dollar's worth of gas. And, it never failed that along with their purchase, they also wanted the full service. To me, it was embarrassing to be seen in public with grease up to my elbows and smudges on my face. I also hated the fact that I could never get the grease out from under my finger nails or out of the pores of the skin of my hands. Car washing was another matter. The cars were so heavily laden with chrome that it was impossible to wash one without getting at least one cut finger or hand. In all the time that I worked at that job, I never wore fewer than six band aids on my hands and fingers.

On certain weekends, when the service center became especially busy, I would be called over to help out in the store. It seemed that I had a natural talent for sales. Well, not really. As it happened, a goodly percentage of the customers were hill people from the surrounding rural areas. And, being a hillbilly myself, I spoke their language. So, it did not take long for me to establish their trust and, before I knew it, I became the top sales person. After doing tune-ups, pumping gas and washing cars for a year, I was offered the job of assistant manager of the service center and given a sizeable raise to come in every weekend and on any evening that I could spare from homework or classes.

My experiences at the gas station convinced me that – if I ever reached the point in life where I made enough money – I would never again wash another car or do another tune-up. To me, two of the greatest inventions of all times were the drive-through car wash and the computerized, fuel-injected engine.

Little did I expect that years later and long after I stopped washing my own cars by hand, Elmer would pull into my driveway with his car's engine missing something awful. He pulled up, got out and said, “Hey Ken, do yuh know anything about cars?” “Uh oh,” I thought, “here it comes.” My reply was, “Sorry Elmer, about all I know about them is how to drive them.” Elmer said, “Mines acting up – take a look at it for me.” I tried real hard not to, with comments like, “Elmer, I really don’t know anything about cars.” But, as usual, Elmer was more persistent than me and used just the right words to con me, like “well, just take a look at it for me – you’re better at spotting things than me.” What could I do? I had him turn off the engine and I raised the hood. The first thing I did was put my hand on the distributor cap and discovered that his distributor was loose. Well, loose distributors are pretty easy to fix. I dug my timing light out of the closet in the garage and rummaged around until I found my auto manual so I could look up the timing setting. I marked the fly wheel and hooked up the timing light. I then had Elmer start his car and I turned the distributor until the timing light showed that it was where it should be. I tightened the bolt on the distributor and had him turn off and restart the engine. The engine started on the first turn and ran smoothly. Elmer got a big grin on his face. “I knew you could do er. I told Lizzie – if anyone can fix it, Ken Miller can. Now I can go take her for groceries.”

The next morning, Elmer popped over with a bag of fresh-picked sweet corn, a cantaloupe and a dozen tomatoes from his garden. “Here, Lizzie was so happy with the car that she got up early and picked these for you. She said that car never ran that good in all the time we had it. She told me that from now on, no one touches that car except Ken Miller. And, you let him look at any of your other motors that aren’t working right too.”

The Bird's Nest

I AM STILL NOT SURE why but, it seemed like every time Elmer needed help with something it was always at a most inconvenient time for me. One spring week, Carole and I had been looking forward to the weekend. A shoe factory in a town about 30 miles east of where we lived had been remodeled into an art gallery with about 40 individual galleries in it and, we planned to spend all day Saturday touring the galleries. And, for the following day, I had plans of spending the day trout fishing on Manada Creek. At breakfast on Saturday morning, we were discussing what time we should leave. Since the galleries opened at 10:00 AM, we felt that if we left around 9:30 that would get us there about the time they opened their doors. That was the plan. We would spend several hours touring the galleries and have a nice relaxing lunch in the little restaurant they also opened in the factory. After we completed our visit to the galleries, we would spend some time in the farmer's market next door. They always had some great locally grown fruits, vegetables, meats and, especially, those wonderful Pennsylvania Dutch baked goods like shoofly pie and whoopie pies. It was going to be a relaxing and enjoyable day.

At 8:30, the phone rang and Carole answered it. I couldn't tell who she was talking to or what she was talking about as the conversation was choppy with half comments like, "Well, how did that happen?" and, "Well, uh," Well, er, I think - How long? When did? Well sure but, Okay, he'll be over." When she hung up the phone she told me that I had to go over and help Elmer remove a bird's nest from his corn picker. "What in the world are you talking about?" I asked. "Elmer said the starlings built a nest in his corn picker and he needs you to help him get it out," was her reply. "Carole, I haven't had a shower yet and we're leaving for the galleries in an hour. I can't go over there and help Elmer take a bird's nest out of his corn picker!" "Why can't he just take it out himself?" I asked. "He said it was down in and he couldn't reach it. I told him you'd be right over," She said, and then added, "How long could it take you to get a little bird's nest out of a corn picker?" "Go give him a hand and we will still have plenty of time to get to the galleries."

So, I got my car out of the garage and drove over to Elmer's. When I got there, I found him standing by the corn picker with an adjustable wrench in his hand. "Them darn starlings got into my corn picker and built a nest. It's too deep for me to reach, if you can help me get this bolt off, I should be able to reach er and pull er out," was my greeting. Well, it turned out that when Elmer last used the corn picker in the fall, he had gotten a bunch of corn stalks, fox-tailed grasses and mud jammed up inside the escalator that carries the corn ears up and into the hopper after they are separated from the corn stalks. This just didn't look like a job that could be done in any short period of time. The bolt that Elmer wanted me to remove for him was so banged up from his efforts that I would have to hack-saw it off and replace it. Besides, it was obvious that when the jam occurred, he had broken off several of the paddles that push the corn ears up the escalator. Additionally, there were several other paddles that looked like they had been missing for a long time. "Elmer, why do you need this thing fixed today - you don't have any corn to pick?" I asked him. "Yep, I do. There's about a half acre in the back field that I couldn't get picked last fall before the snows came. I need to pick it so I can plow it today to get ready to plant some barley," was his explanation.

Well, since I couldn't talk Elmer into a postponement of the project, I decided to bite the bullet and get the job done. It took about two hours to get the panels off the escalator of the corn picker so we could get in and dig out the jam. Things were so tightly packed and the dried mud had turned everything into something akin to home-made bricks that it took us about another hour to chip and pry everything out. Once we got the obstruction cleared away, we discovered that the escalator chain had broken and would need to be repaired. I asked Elmer if he had any spare links for the chain and he assured me he had some down in his garage. His garage is a walk-in nightmare that is half filled with boxes, crates, cans, bags, palettes, spare roofing shingles, baling twine, fertilizers, weed killers and spare parts that have been removed from equipment or awaiting replacement on equipment. After rummaging around through boxes and drawers for about an hour, Elmer declared, "Here they are, I knowed I had them."

So, we got the escalator chain repaired, oiled, greased and working fine. Then it was apparent that about half of paddles needed to be replaced before the picker would work efficiently. By now, it was about one o'clock in the afternoon. And, since Elmer didn't have any replacement wooden paddles for the escalator, I had to go home to my shop and make them. When I got home, Carole asked me where I had been so long and, how had I gotten so dirty. "Don't talk to me," I told her. "You're the one who got me into this mess." "Well, I didn't realize it was going to be an all day affair! How long does it take to remove one little starling nest?" was her reply. "What do you want me to do?" I need to make him new paddles before we can put the corn picker back together so he can go pick corn," I asked. "How much longer is this going to take?" she asked. "Probably another two hours," was my reply. "Well, go get it done. We can go to the galleries tomorrow!" she said.

At about 4:00 PM, I returned home dirty, greasy, tired and dripping blood from two cut knuckles. But, I had the satisfaction of seeing Elmer go by on his tractor with his corn picker in tow, headed for the back field.

As I walked in the door, Carole said, "You better go straight to the shower and be careful you don't sit on anything, you're awfully dirty." I'll get some dinner started. We can go to the galleries tomorrow." As I headed for the shower, I said, "Tomorrow I am supposed to be fishing Manada Creek." Her retort was, "You can go fishing any time. If you hadn't spent all day helping Elmer, we would have made it to the galleries today. Now, we'll just have to do it tomorrow!"

The Chain Saw

WELL, IT LOOKED LIKE it was going to be an ideal weekend, especially for some trout fishing. My friend, Lou, and I had planned a trip to the cabin for the weekend so we could fish Penn's Creek. Shortly before lunch on Friday, I called Lou to see what time I could expect him. He felt that he could get off from work a bit early and be at my house by about 6:00 PM. This would work out fine as we could stop at the grocery store on the way to the cabin and buy whatever extra food we would need for the weekend. It was early May, the ideal time for insects to be coming off Penn's Creek and for maximum trout activity. It was going to be a most enjoyable weekend.

By 5:00 PM I had everything assembled that I would be taking with me, fishing gear, clothing, reading materials, etc. I was just going over a mental checklist to assure that I had not forgotten anything when Carole called to tell me that Lizzie was on the telephone. When I answered the phone, Lizzie said, "Ken, Elmer wants you to stop over and help him get his chain saw started." When I told her that I was about to leave for the cabin, she relayed this message to Elmer who told her to tell me it would only take a few minutes. "He really needs to cut some limbs off the maple tree outside cause they are rubbing against the house." What could I do? How could I turn down a request from Lizzie? Elmer certainly knew that I couldn't refuse Lizzie. That is why he had her call me whenever he wanted to make sure I would respond to his request. I finally conceded and told her that I would stop over as soon as Lou arrived. A few minutes later, Lou pulled into the driveway. When I told him we had to go over and help Elmer get this chain saw started, his reply was, "Well, there goes Penn's Creek!" "No," I said. "Elmer assures me this will only take a few minutes." "We will see," was his reply.

When we got over to Elmer's, he had the chain saw waiting for us. However, no amount of pulling on the starter rope would cause the thing to start. "When did you last run this thing?" I asked Elmer. "Waal, I used it last fall to trim some brushes," was his reply. "It sounds like the carburetor is gummed up," I said. "Yep, I thought so," he replied. "Here, I bought this carburetor kit, so all we need to do is take it apart, put it back together and it should work fine," he stated. "Elmer, I don't know anything about rebuilding chain saw carburetors," I told him. "You kin do er," he said. "If you could fix the carburetor on my car, you can fix this little thing," he said. Well, no arguments to the contrary were acceptable so, I finally relented and said, "OK, Elmer. I will give it a shot but I am making no guarantees."

We spread newspapers over Lizzie's kitchen table and went to work on the chain saw. To begin with, the thing needed a thorough cleaning as every nook and cranny of it was jamb-packed with sawdust that was mixed with oil and grease. So, considerable time was spent cleaning out this gunk so we could locate the nuts, bolts and screws that we would need to deal with to take it apart. When I pulled the protective housing off the chain bar sprocket, a spring shot across the room. Fortunately, we were able to locate and retrieve it. My hands were a little shaky as I began removing the screws that would release the carburetor. Along about then, Elmer got out a half-gallon of J&B® Scotch. "Here," he said, you will need a little nip to git your attention focused." "Okay," I said just a little one is all I want." Well, Elmer's idea of a little one is not a shot. He didn't even own a shot glass. His glasses were originally jelly jars and, he filled them three-quarters full before passing them around.

The carburetor turned out, as expected, to be gunked up and in need of cleaning. However, by the time we had it cleaned and reassembled, the table was still littered with parts from the disassembled chain saw and the jelly glasses were empty. When Elmer offered a refill, Lou said, "Why not? It's already dark out and by the time we get this thing back together it will be too late to head for the cabin tonight." By the time we got the chain saw reassembled, it was getting close to midnight and I was seeing double of everything. The level in the J&B® bottle had dropped considerably. When the last screw was tightened, we discovered that there were only one screw and a small spring left over. Hopefully, they were extras from the carburetor repair kit as I had no intention of taking the chain saw apart again. We bid Elmer a goodnight and told him not to attempt starting the chain saw until morning. Lou and I decided to let the car parked and walk home.

The next morning, we awoke knowing we were going to pay a price for our transgression of the night before. Neither of us felt like going fishing and neither of us felt like making the two-hour drive up to the cabin. So, we decided to just sort of lounge around all weekend. As we were drinking our first cups of coffee, Lizzie called to tell us that Elmer wanted us to know that the chain saw had started on the first pull and that he was already out cutting limbs off the maple tree. She added, "He says to tell you that when you get some time, stop over and take a look at his roto tiller."

On Sunday afternoon, Lou headed home early. We agreed that come the next weekend we would make it up to the cabin. Before he backed down the driveway, he said, "If Elmer calls next Friday, have Carole tell him you went up to the cabin on Thursday!"

Shades of Willard

Elmer's farm has 126 acres. It abuts several other farms of similar size. Apparently one of his farming neighbors had been using a ravine at the back of his farm as a garbage dump. This led to a rat explosion and, since this ravine was not too far from the back boundary of Elmer's farm some of the rats migrated to Elmer's barn.

One Saturday morning, Elmer stopped at my house to ask me if I owned a 22 rifle. Of course, I did. He asked me to bring the rifle over after it got dark and help him get rid of some rats that had invaded his barn. When I asked him why, all of a sudden, he developed a rat problem, he told me about the dump on the neighbor's farm and how the rats from there had migrated to Elmer's barn. To a country boy, there's nothing more entertaining that shooting rats! So, I readily agreed to come over after dark and give him a hand.

That evening, when I was getting ready to leave, Carole asked me where I was going with a gun. I knew that if I told her I was going over to shoot rats in Elmer's barn, I would get a grilling that would hold me up. So, I simply told her that Elmer had asked me to stop over and bring my gun. She gave me a skeptical look but didn't say more.

When I got out of my car, Elmer met me in the driveway and handed me a hand-full of 22 bird shot cartridges. These cartridges contain leaded shot that is as fine as grains of table salt. They are quite safe to use inside a barn as they expend the bulk of their energy after traveling only 6 to 10 feet. Being of lead, they are not penetrating enough to puncture water lines if they are accidentally hit but they are powerful enough to penetrate a rat's hide and kill it.

My rifle was a single shot. I loaded it and Elmer told me to follow him and be ready to shoot. In the dark, we gently pushed open the door to the stable, far enough so that we could enter. Elmer leaned over and whispered, "Get ready, I'm going to turn on the flashlight – you'll see a bunch in that corner just in front of you." Elmer turned on the flashlight and my skin immediately began to crawl. My immediate thought was that I had stepped onto the set of the movie, *Willard*. There were rats running everywhere! In the corner, in front of me, there were at least a dozen, all crawling over each other trying to find an escape route. I aimed and shot and that added to the chaos! One rat even started climbing my pant leg – fortunately, on the outside. I knocked it off with the gun barrel and immediately began loading the gun again. Egads! I sure wished I had something other than a single shot rifle! Nevertheless, over the next hour or so, we dispensed with 28 rats. Sunday night, I returned and we repeated the process. However, this time, I had tied my pants legs shut so no rats could get inside if they suddenly decided that my pants legs looked like a promising escape route.

On Monday, at noon, I stopped by the local gun shop near my house to see what they had that would better arm me in this newfound battle. What they had was a nine-shot 22 caliber pistol. I bought it and stopped off to show it to Elmer. "That ought to do the trick," he said. "See you tonight after it gits dark." That night, we set a new record, with 54 rats. On subsequent nights, we came close to but never bettered that one night total. By fall, we were having trouble finding rats. When we turned on the flashlights in the dark, the mad scurrying was gone. The barn was quiet again. Elmer's tally sheet indicated that we had cleaned a total of nearly 1800 rats from his barn. No hunting safari could have ever come close to the hunting excitement we had shared in Elmer's barn that summer. And, fortunately, it never happened again as the neighbor was forced to clean up the mess he had created and cease and desist with his landfill disposal operation.

Elmer, Carole and the Milk Cans

THE WEATHER WARMED CONSIDERABLY for a day in March in the Northeast and I took advantage of this by cleaning up the leaves that had blown onto the back patio. When I was done, Carole suggested that I hook up a garden hose and wash down the patio. Unfortunately, this required that I turn on the outside faucet that I had drained in the fall in preparation for freezing weather. It also required that I make a visit to the storage facility that I was renting to retrieve a garden hose. But, it was a nice day with the temperatures in the high 50s and I needed the exercise. So, I drove over to the storage facility to get a hose. When I opened the garage door to it I saw the hose reels sitting there behind the maroon milk cans. I moved the milk cans out and retrieved the hose reel that I wanted. I then put the milk cans back, closed and locked the door. For some reason, as I was driving home, the sight of those milk cans popped into my head and I began to wonder why I had kept them for all those many years. It was then that I recalled where they came from and why I was still keeping them.

One Sunday, not too long after moving into our house, Elmer, as he usually did on Sundays, stopped by for a visit. He, Carole and I were sitting on the front porch chatting about whatever came to mind. At one point in the conversation, Carole asked Elmer if he knew where she could buy two milk cans. Elmer's reply was, "What the hang you planning to do, buy a cow?" "No," was her reply, "I want to paint them and put one on each side of the front door as decorations." "I just might have what you want," Elmer told her. "So, don't go buying any till I have a chance to look around."

Two days later Carole received her milk cans. And, it was a good thing that she was not planning on buying a cow because those milk cans would never again hold milk. There were holes rusted through the bottoms and both had multiple dents and a healthy coating of rust. But to Carole, they were beautiful and she immediately got busy removing the rust. She then gave both cans two coats of rust preventative paint followed by a final coat of maroon paint to match our front doors. She then added some pears and flowers like she had learned to paint in the toll painting class she was taking. I had to admit, when they were done, they looked pretty good and they made attractive additions on each side of our front door.

A few years went by and Carole decided that a change was needed out front and so, the milk cans had to go. However, since they had been given to her by Elmer, they could not go far. They were simply moved from the front door to the back door where they remained for several more years before being moved to the garage. The problem with moving things to the garage is that once you get in the habit, you soon discover that you no longer have room for the car. After I built the barn, the milk cans were moved to the barn. But I soon discovered that barns, like garages, are never big enough to hold everything you want to put in them. So, a major cleaning out was necessary. When I asked Carole if it would be okay for me to now dispose of the milk cans, she replied, "Elmer gave me those cans so, I would like to keep them."

It is funny how some of us are natural born pack rats and cannot bring ourselves to part with certain things that we no longer have a use for, such as the milk cans or dog cages that we use only once every eight years or so when we decide it is time to get a new puppy. Or, the oriental rugs that no longer match the décor of our home or the fall decorations for the front lawn or the outdoor lights that no longer work – or the mountain of other things we save although they no longer have a use or a very limited use once each year.

We have been storing those milk cans for nearly thirty years. Why? Because Elmer gave them to Carole and Carole won't let me get rid of them because they were a gift from Elmer. I expect that one day our heirs will hold an auction to get rid of all the left-over things in the garage, the attic, the barn and the storage facility. And someone will say, "I wonder why they kept those rusty old milk cans all these years?"

Elmer

They are Biting on the Swatty

As I LOOKED OUT over his farm this morning I found myself thinking, "Boy, I sure miss fishing with that old guy." Once Elmer discovered that I liked to go fishing he was forever asking me "when are we gonna go fishing?" Most of the time he would call and say "Merle, or Lemuel, or Samuel, or Lizzie's brother, or whoever, called and said they are really biting at the Middletown Reservoir or at Falmouth (or wherever). Let's go there." Elmer was the type who, when the urge to go fishing struck, he wanted to go right then and there. It didn't matter to Elmer that I was only half through mowing the grass or that I was in the middle of taking the shutters down to paint them. When the urge struck, he was ready to go. For years it looked like I only ever half finished most of the projects I started around my home.

Elmer loved fishing. But, Elmer wasn't the greatest fisherman! He was forever getting snagged and saying, "Ken, can you help me out here?" I would no sooner get him un-snagged than he would throw right into the same spot and we would repeat the process all over again. Elmer never did develop a knack for fishing with artificial lures. For him, a night crawler and a big bobber were the only things to use. Also, Elmer wasn't terribly adept at catching night crawlers. So, every time it rained, I would be out in the evening searching my yard with a flashlight for a supply of night crawlers for Elmer. For, "sure as shootin", every time it rained Elmer knew the fish would be biting the next day and, I could expect his call. On lakes I got blisters rowing him around. He always thought the fish were biting on the other side of the lake where he could see "that other boat." "That's where they must be biting if those guys are over there," he would say. As soon as we got across the lake, he would notice a boat on the side we had just left. "That's where they must be biting if those guys are over there," he would again say. On lakes, I spent all my time rowing and had little time for fishing. Often in the spring I slipped and fell into icy streams trying to get Elmer's line untangled. When the fish were biting, it was a great day. When they weren't, it was my fault for not taking him over to where they were biting. My fishing outings with Elmer were akin to taking a little kid fishing for the first time. He never quite got the hang of it but he sure enjoyed reeling in the occasional fish. I don't recall ever coming back from fishing with Elmer without saying to my wife "that's it, I've had it, I'll never go fishing with Elmer again." A week would pass and Elmer would call and say "Billy says they are really biting up on Stony Creek, when can we go?" And, off we would go again.

Elmer died several years ago at the ripe old age of 89. Now, every time it rains I still get the urge to go out in my back yard and look for night crawlers. In spite of all the frustration I experienced trying to fish with Elmer, he was one of my best friends and I would love to have him call me up just once more and say "hey, Marvin says they are really biting on the Swatty."